W22

JOY YEARS

JOY YEARS

My Retirement Memoir

ROBERT WARREN CROMEY

JOY YEARS
MY RETIREMENT MEMOIR

iUniverse books may be ordered through booksellers or by contacting:

iUniverse
1663 Liberty Drive
Bloomington, IN 47403
www.iuniverse.com
1-800-Authors (1-800-288-4677)

ISBN: 978-1-5320-3487-9 (sc)
ISBN: 978-1-5320-3488-6 (e)

Print information available on the last page.

iUniverse rev. date: 12/22/2017

"I endorse Robert Cromey's book …."

- Elizabeth Ann Cromey

I dedicate this book to my wife
Elizabeth Ann Cromey
with thanks for all her love.

I want to acknowledge and thank
the late Michelle Schmidt, who encouraged my writing
and Pamela Portugal Walatka for her copy
editing and many wise suggestions.

JOY YEARS

I love being retired. I loved my work as a priest of the Episcopal Church, especially the last twenty years as rector of Trinity Church, San Francisco. I enjoyed being a preacher, teacher, celebrant at the Eucharist, liturgist, administrator, and fundraiser. Weddings, funerals, baptisms, visiting in hospitals or in people's homes, and counseling the confused and the bereaved were moving and gave rich variety to my life and work as a priest.

In 1983 Ann and I married at Trinity, followed by a grand reception and by now a thirty-three-year wonderful marriage. Ann was a loving support to my ministry and delightful human being. The people of Trinity loved Ann far more than they loved me. She dressed beautifully, was famous for her hats and was warm and loving to all. I on the other hand was a bit abrupt, had to say no sometimes, and made decisions that some people did not like. However, most of the time I felt I was beloved and respected as leader and rector.

At this writing I have been retired for fifteen years. I have thoroughly enjoyed these years and have learned a lot about retirement and myself. I continue to grow in accepting every part of my humanity. My body, sexuality, and mind have grown and diminished over the years. I have learned more and more to be thankful for Ann, my daughters and grandchildren, friends, and the new people that I meet. I am a loyal but critical citizen of the United

States. I continue to learn how to use the valuable time and leisure I have been given.

I realize that I have to find meaning for my life from within myself. Family, church, hobbies, and friends do not provide that inner satisfaction. It must come from within. On the other hand, family, church, hobbies, and friends nourish that inner self. I believe that inner self-satisfaction comes from God. I sense something far greater than myself, a sense of transcendence, wonder, mystery about the world. Acknowledging that which I call God renders me that gift of inner peace and certainty.

In this memoir of my retirement years, I want to share with you, dear reader, something of who I am, what I do, what I think about and have learned in these joyful years since I retired.

CONTENTS

CHAPTER 1

RETIRED

The day after the splendid last Sunday as rector of Trinity, Ann and I flew to Puerto Vallarta Mexico where we had spent Presidents week for some years. The warm, moist air relaxes the body immediately. With change and heat, our muscles sag and we relax. Puerto Vallarta is a tropical large town where we rest, read, walk, and do little else. We always enjoy PV with its mix of tourism and local people gathering and walking along the Malecon in the warm evenings. We have stayed in a lovely condominium overlooking the colorful town and the blue of the bay. I reflected on the warm feelings about our send-off and the love and affection expressed to us by our many friends and parishioners.

The first thing I did when we got home was make a new calling card for myself on the computer and printer. It read:

Robert Warren Cromey
Pensioner

No address, no phone number. I was all ready for my new life as an unemployed man. I hate the cliché, "I am so busy in retirement, I have no idea how I had time enough to work." I choose what I want to do. Sure, I have to do some things like shop, cook, eat, shower, shave, and take care of Ann. But I truly choose to do those things, I love to do them. It gives me pleasure to shop, I actually enjoy the process of food shopping. I don't dawdle, I go and get what I want but I do enjoy the stores: the products, fruit, vegetables, fish, and meat. I like to look at them and I like to eat them.

Choice is wonderful. I was invited to preach in other churches from time to time and enjoyed the preparation, delivery of sermons, and the response afterward. But when Sunday night comes, I realize I did not have to begin to prepare another sermon for the next Sunday. I really like that feeling of relief and no pressure. I get to preach and celebrate the Eucharist just enough to keep myself connected to the ongoing liturgical life of the Episcopal Church.

I awaken each morning in San Francisco and feel full of strength and energy. That goes until after lunch when I tire and take a nap. I start the day by making coffee, turning on the heat, getting the paper, drinking the coffee, reading the paper, making love with Ann (every other morning), having breakfast, and getting Ann off to school. I settle down to chores at my desk. I do the bookkeeping, pay bills, attempt the checkbook reconciliation, and write a letter to an editor.

My first real project was to begin to write a memoir. Certainly my life and work have been interesting and the issues I stand for have been important in church and state. My ego is definitely involved, I want to be known, regarded, seen as significant, and to tell the world how wonderful I am. Now I know few people in the world really care all that much about my life story but I want it to be there anyway for all to read if they want to. Besides I just want to do it. So I started soon after I retired.

I chose to emulate other writers and write every day for an hour or so. The writing was easy and I enjoyed and felt sad and glad about all the memories that emerged. I plugged away at it for two years.

Having more free time and fewer things I have to do, I have more time to think about items of importance that I touched on fleetingly in my working life. Death, the divorce, and the children for instance.

I think about my own death every day. I don't want a lot of pain so I hope my dying will be brief and pain-free. I hope friends and family will do all they can to assure that I do not live a long painful dying process. I hope that some friend, doctor, or drug user will hasten my departure if it looks like I will linger in pain and helplessness.

I do not fear the death itself. The end is the end and I hope for a resurrection, as is part of my Christian faith. The hope of the resurrection means some future contact with family and friends who have died or will die after I do. I'd love to see my mother and father again and so many friends who have already died. I have no illusions that this will happen but I hope it does.

I worry that Ann will suffer a great deal when I die. It will be hard for her to recover and resume a new life without me but of course she will. I feel sad that I will not be there to comfort her. If the dead miss the living in any way I shall be in torment without her.

My daughters will have some pain and sorrow but will move on nicely without their part-time, far-away Dad. I also hope I don't die in a way that shocks and horrifies Ann, like dying while taking a nap and she discovers my body, or that I am injured and disfigured and she must identify my maimed corpse.

I think about suicide only if I would find myself in great pain or greatly incapacitated. I don't have access yet to drugs that could kill me swiftly and mercifully. I must do something about that. I could not take a gun to my head or jump from a bridge or under a train or bus. I have no impulse along those lines. I am too much of a coward anyway.

When I think of death and dying every day for a bit, it is not interfering with my life and functioning, but the thought springs to mind from time to time. That is certainly part of the business of having less pressure on my mind in connection with work, schedules, writing sermons, visiting the sick, and doing parish administration.

I have completed my funeral plan and we have made our wills so those items are in order. That reminds me that both need to be revisited and worked on a bit to make sure they reflect what we really think now. As I like to say I have a hundred hymns chosen for my funeral and I have to chop the list down to three or four at most.

Shortly after we returned from PV, I went to visit Carol Craven, a woman I had a date with in the 70's. She had red hair, freckles, was quite pretty and funny. She had multiple sclerosis, which I knew about when I first met her. The date was pleasant but we didn't click. I had not seen her for twenty-five years. She was in a nursing home quite crippled and disabled with advanced stages of MS. She could not talk, and could move only a little on her own. She had to be fed and cared for in all ways. She wanted to see me as she had been in a group of mine and we had had our one date.

She was glad to see me as her eyes brightened and she became rather agitated when I came in with Joan, a mutual friend. She was basically still attractive but so very ill and helpless. I talked about my life and Ann and the church and she listened and could not reply. After about an hour I left. A few weeks after my visit, Carol's parents took her to the South where she was from and no word was left as to where she had gone. I have no idea if she is still alive.

Talk about helpless, that is the way I felt and still feel when I see Carol or anyone so sick and disabled by the dreaded MS. The sense of helplessness haunts me. I'd so hate to be in that state. Planning and buying long-term health insurance was hard for me as I had to look at the fact that maybe someday I would have to be cared for like Carol had to be. I have been in enough nursing homes visiting parishioners to know how much I would hate having to be there. Visiting Carol was a grim reminder of what could happen to me, to Ann, my daughters, and their families.

Fromm Institute for Life-long Learning

Before I retired I had taken a writing course at the Fromm Institute for Life Long Learning situated on the campus of the University of San Francisco. I took the course and enjoyed the assignments and the actual writing and especially reading my pieces out loud. I always like to show off and usually my pieces were funny and often insightful.

The other people's writing was often interesting and poignant. We had one or two people who had survived the holocaust. One guy had a smart answer for everything the teacher said and never let a class go by without mentioning he had been a survivor. He had also recently lost his wife. Such a strange mix of feeling I had for him. He was annoyingly trying to be funny and talked a lot, so I wanted to kill him. Then I felt sad for him that he had been in the awful camps, and then I'd feel annoyed that he mentioned the camps at least once in each class. I wanted to tell him to shut up but never did. I did tell him I was sad that his wife had died and thought to myself how horrible it would be if Ann died and I was left alone.

As I looked around the room at the other members of my class and then at lunch seeing all these old people, I realized I did not want to be identified with them. They were all so old, so very old. Then I realized I was probably older than most of them. As I am always interested in women particularly, I noticed there were no women whom I found sexually attractive. Too large, too wrinkled, too soft, too gray, too passive, too boring, and some too aggressive and dominating.

I noted one woman, slender, beautifully dressed, very reserved, and never spoke in class nor did she seem to have any acquaintances that she spoke with. She was lovely to look at, may have been younger than most and had an air of mystery about her. I never spoke with her either.

I found the men fit the same description as the women. Often they were show offs when asking questions or making comments. I met and enjoyed Steve Spellman and we often had lunch together and still do. He is an attractive, retired, insurance manager and had worked for the State of California government for a while. He is a liberal, married and lives in Alameda. He asked me what Bible he might buy in order to read the Bible all the way through. I referred him to the Revised Standard Version with short history and commentary to go along with it. He did read the Bible all the way through and he seemed more relieved than glad he had finished it.

The one piece I wrote that caused a storm of controversy was about being tired of hearing about the holocaust all the time. One man told me I had no right to read such an article in class. One woman countered that we all should listen to whatever we want to write. One man insisted I was an anti-Semite. Most people said nothing. Several people after class said they too were tired of endless talk about that terrible crime against humanity.

I tried a few of the lecture classes at the Fromm, one on James Joyce's Ulysses and others on opera and baroque music. Too much talk and not enough music. I get bored with the lectures, hated the dumb questions people asked and the inane comments made by some just trying to show off. I should talk. I have resolved to attend writing classes and small group seminars that interest me. The Fromm does a great job but it doesn't fit my peculiar personality.

Sacraments for Evangelism

We in the church can help bring the sacraments—particularly Baptism, Holy Matrimony, and Holy Communion—to the people before they are ready to come to the church. We Episcopalians need to open up our minds to see the sacraments as tools for evangelism. Some in the church seem to think we need to protect the sacraments from the unwashed. The Book of Common Prayer and the canons of the church assume the church is a 19th century English village. The fact is that we, the church, operate in a global village.

Some churches in Southern California advertise Baptism for anyone who wants it, no questions asked, no preparation necessary. Dozens of people show up for the Easter Eve rite. Trinity San Francisco does weddings for forty couples a year. The couple receives counseling. The church ministers to the couple and their family at the most important moment in their lives. If non-members-become members fine. If not, the church is seen as caring and interested in people's lives.

Baptisms in Portugal

In the summer of 2002 I was invited to Cascais, Portugal to baptize the children of a man who was an Anglican and his wife a lapsed Roman Catholic. In addition there were children of ex-patriate American, English, Dutch, and German lapsed Christians. They live outside of Lisbon in a loosely connected community.

They had explored other churches. The Roman Catholic and Evangelical parishes were too conservative, hide-bound and rule-laden. The Anglican Church near Lisbon was too stuffy and irrelevant to their lives. They wanted their children to be baptized into the Christian Church even though they seldom went to church. The parents had a yearning to incorporate their children in something larger and more spiritual than their family and community. One mother told me that it was her ten-year-old son, Ollie, who wanted to be baptized.

Nadine Scott, an Episcopalian from California, living in Portugal, remembered me from the sixties and thought I'd be liberal enough to do the baptisms. My wife and I were spending six weeks in Paris anyway. I agreed. Ann and I flew from Paris to Lisbon where I held a two-hour preparation session with the parents and Godparents, and an hour-long session with the children the day before the ceremony.

I spoke frankly with the parents and suggested that since they were not about to join a local church, that their family was the church. It was up to them to teach the children how to follow Jesus, pray, read the Bible, and bring the children up in accordance with Christian principles. I suggested the adults might get together to learn how to develop their own religious practices and teach the children. I spoke about the need for worship and the Christian life as characterized by love, compassion, justice, forgiveness, and community.

The children ranged from three to 14 years old with most between seven and ten. I asked them to tell us what they thought of when they thought of water. Bathing, cleaning, swimming, necessary for life were some of the answers given. One little girl said she preferred milk. I stressed that by having the water poured on them they became a member of the Christian Church. The water symbolized that no matter what you do wrong, you can always ask for forgiveness and cleansing. Baptism assures you that God's Holy Spirit is always with you. Some of the children may have learned something from all that.

7

On Sunday in Nadine's lovely back yard, we held the service. Each child stepped forward accompanied by parents and Godparents. I poured some water gently on their foreheads and named the child and said, "I baptize you in the name of the Father, the Son, and the Holy Spirit and welcome you in into God's holy church." We welcomed the children into the church with warm applause.

People also wanted to receive the sacrament of Holy Communion. I broke the bread and blessed the wine with the words of institution. The bread was passed among the people and also some cups of wine. Everyone so moved was welcome to partake of the sacrament.

We then had some time for intercessions and people to speak. Many were moved by the miracle of ritual and quiet. Others hadn't taken communion since childhood. More said they finally saw a connection between baptism and communion and living one's life.

There is a hunger in the lands of western culture for meaning, interconnection, ritual, ceremony, a sense of the sacred and holiness. Parish churches at their best provide all those elements. Parishes have a culture and way of being that does not appeal to everyone. Some churches have driven members away by preaching against all sex outside of marriage, alcohol, birth control, abortion, and dancing. Churches are seen as fostering child molesters, catering to greed and racial segregation. They appear to be anti-intellectual, anti-inquiry, and anti-science. Liturgies are dull and sermons unconnected to real life. Many people are floundering in their search for ultimate meaning that we find in God.

In Acts 8:34-40 we have the story of the Ethiopian eunuch. He hears Philip preach and wants to be baptized. He was a gentile, black, and unable to bear children. He was immediately baptized. No classes, no promises, no rules or canons stood in the way of his immediate baptism.

The people in Portugal are intelligent, sensitive, hardworking, and prosperous. They expressed a real need for baptism for their children. They are not sure what to do with their newfound connection to a religious experience. We in the church can help bring the sacraments— particularly Baptism, Holy Matrimony, and

Holy Communion—to the people before they are ready to come to the church. Perhaps many will turn out to be active communicants after all.

After My Retirement

The Episcopal Church has a ludicrous policy of asking a vacant parish to do a yearlong study of what the parish thinks it wants in a new rector. That is fine if the there is a solid base of members and a good income. Many churches, like Trinity had a small base core and a slim budget. To leave the church without a strong leader for a year more means that old members die or drift away and no new members fill their shoes. The rigidity of the bishops causes Trinity and others to flounder and run into serious troubles.

After Trinity Paid off two short-term rectors, the church had to become a mission rather than a parish. It could no longer support a full-time rector. Trinity and St. Peter's Church began discussing a merger.

CHAPTER 2

AGING

Some thoughts on aging written by others

Age does not depend on years, but on temperament and health.

Age is a high price to pay for maturity.

Embrace and love old age. It abounds with pleasure if you know how to use it.

Age is not a particularly interesting subject. Anyone can get old. All you have to do is live long enough.

My thoughts on aging

I learned from my time at Esalen Institute in 1968 to pay attention to my body. I had never thought of that before. In group therapy, we looked carefully at our bodies. We talked about what we liked and disliked about our hair, eyes, noses, ears, breasts, bellies, pubes, penises, legs, arms, and feet. Except for sex, pain, or vanity I seldom had paid any attention to my body.

Now that I am 86, I still look at my body. Maybe, more so now that my aging body demands more of my attention. I look in the mirror and wonder who that is looking back at me. I look like I am 86 years old but I think of myself as thirty.

The fact is that my face is full of hills and valleys that I have noticed more and more over the years. All of us look worn and weathered as we age. My swimmer's strong chest muscles are not only sagging but also wrinkled. I have brown spots on my hands. Where in hell did those come from? I really don't care to know. A couple of my fingers are crooked and hurt sometimes. My fingernails look better than ever, as I get a manicure regularly.

My hands can't easily open plastic bags, screw tops, or pull the rings to open cans of beer. Thank God for screw tops on the Simi Sauvignon Blanc wine we enjoy. Scotch, gin, and bourbon tops still open easily. Good Grip can openers, peelers, and kitchen utensils make for easier handling. I also feel and am clumsy a lot.

I have always had trouble with my feet and legs. As a fast-growing teen, I fell over my feet a lot. I was pigeon-toed. X-rays told my parents and me that one hip was higher than the other. I can't remember which one. I got blisters on my feet when I played basketball in high school. After exercise running for a number of years, I have had one left hip replacement and each knee replaced with metal and plastic. The hip and one knee were replaced over twenty years ago. I have pain in that aging right knee when I walk up and down stairs. We now have a stair lift that gets me up and down some 35 steps to our flat. I wish to avoid any major surgery on my legs as long as I can. I am fortunate that I have no leg pain while sitting or sleeping.

I take a lot of pills for my blood pressure, heart, stroke prevention, and thyroid, plus drops for glaucoma in my eyes. I am an ideal patient. I do as my doctors tell me to do and take what I am told to take. That's what I pay them for, but more importantly, I trust traditional medicine. There is plenty of opinion that alternative, Chinese, Chiropractic, herbal, and other kinds of medicine work and are helpful. Other people do well combining various healing possibilities. I for one want to stick with the kind that seems to have worked best for me, and that is traditional Western medicine.

My heart has atrial fibrillation, irregular patterns of beating. I take prescribed medicine for it. I very occasionally have light chest pain that disappears quickly. My cardiologist asserts this is a result of some of the drugs I take. She assures me that my heart is OK for a person my age.

I am fortunate that I don't worry much about my health. If I have a problem that I think is important, I consult my doctor. I worry about a number of friends who are unwilling to consult when they have problems.

When I have a crisis about health or have to undergo treatments, I look at surgeries and procedures as just new adventures. This happened a few years ago when I had a cancerous spot on my back. The dreaded cancer word, melanoma, was unpleasant, but the successful surgery to remove it was a thrill.

Cancer caused the deaths of three of my grandparents. So far, I have had some skin cancers scraped from my nose and cheeks. They come from the endless sunbathing I did as a teen and young man trying to look tan and glorious. The skin cancers may also have come from X-ray treatments I got for teen acne.

I have worn eyeglasses since I was in college. I changed prescriptions, lenses and frames over the years as needed. I now have glaucoma in both eyes. The right is worse than my left. I have a life sentence of three drops a day to ward off further degeneration of the optic nerve and macular degeneration.

My hearing is slowly ebbing away. I noticed it first in the early 1980s when I could not hear the coffee grinder alarm clock several rooms away. I started wearing well-hidden and expensive hearing aids about a decade ago. What a nuisance they are as tiny batteries only last a week and they need intricate changing.

Before Christmas 2015, I climbed out of the pool and said to myself, I am not swimming for exercise any more. I was not enjoying it. I found it tedious. Dressing in the morning, driving to the pool, undressing, donning my swim suit, putting on the swim fins, adjusting the goggles, bearing the initial cold shock, and then swimming became a bore. Getting out of the pool, chilly, taking a shower, drying off, getting dressed for the second time that day and driving home became more than I wanted to do. I just did not want to swim any more.

Ann was unhappy, as it was one more thing to hasten my demise. Daughter Sarah said, "Daddy, you've been swimming for 75 years. You can quit if you want to."

Two years ago, I started using a cane to help my balance. My friend Markley Morris in his 70s threw away his cane after hiring a personal trainer for a few months. I started with Evan, the same trainer, in May of 2016.

Evan Mather is my first personal trainer. He helps me get stronger. I want to throw away the cane. I learn to use my body to give me more energy and vitality. The cane is still with me after ten sessions but it may soon be gone. The basic exercises are restoring and strengthening the core muscles of my body. What are the core muscles? Tighten your stomach muscles. That feeling and the muscles that are pulling together when you tighten are a few examples of the core muscle system. While I am lying on my back, then on my stomach, Evan gives me a variety of exercises that strengthen those inner core muscles. Pulleys to the left of me, pulleys to the right of me. One hand, two hands. Sitting, standing are exercises to strengthen me and still be varied enough to keep me interested. I call his studio the torture chamber as he puts my body through many moves and tightening and loosening that sometimes hurt.

Restoring balance is important to me. Lots of standing on one foot and then the other, on the floor and on spongy surfaces strengthens ankles and calves. Those together with core strengthening help my balance.

Evan's enthusiasm, sincerity and patience with my weakness help me push through difficult exercises with willingness. As I am 86 and he is used to working with far younger people, he is very careful to protect me from falling when I get up off the floor. He holds my hands as I attempt to balance when I stand on one foot. He also keeps count. He'll say do 20 of these mini sit-ups. He keeps count and when I have five more to go he counts aloud to the number 20. That is very helpful as I often lose track of the numbers.

He has started me on using weights, both from pulleys but also metal bars. He introduces them to me slowly and is very protective that I do not drop them on myself.

He does use incorrect grammar when he tells me to "lay" down on the mat. Good English is "lie down on the mat, Robert." Ann tells me that it is almost impossible to get people to use the correct form of lie and lay once they have assumed the bad habit for a long time. Ann's line is you have to lie down to get laid.

I do some of the exercises at home for about 20 minutes every other day. I go to Evan's studio once a week for a full hour of exercises.

I am pleasantly astonished how much better I feel since I began. I walk up and down the stairs now and do not use the stair lift much. I feel aliveness in my body. Britt-Marie Ljung, a physician, her husband Warren, and Ann all say that I look better and stronger. I carry the cane often when I am walking. I use it at curbs and dark or crowded places on the streets.

I do wonder if these exercises will do much good in the long run. Is my 85-year-old body really going to improve, strengthen, or develop? My hope is that the workouts will help keep me from breaking bones and getting weaker and keep me as healthy as possible as I age.

I like my body and am grateful for the pleasure it gives me. The sweet satisfactions of sex and the sensation of taste when I eat excite me. As I age my sense of taste diminishes some; thus, I like spicy foods a lot more than I used to. I love the things I can see with my eyes: art, sculpture, the female nude, green grass, and the sea stretching to the horizon. I love the sound of music, Ann's voice, a crackling fire in the fireplace, the sound of silence. I enjoy touching food as I prepare it. I love the feel of human flesh in a handshakes, caresses, hugs, and kisses.

Women and men have surgery on their faces to keep them

looking young. I want to look the way I look. I want to be authentic and real. Of course, people are free to do what they want with their faces for whatever reason. Except to repair disfigurement, I don't think taxpayers should pay the bill for so-called beauty enhancement.

Our society shames people who are fat, skinny or misshapen. People hate the way they look. People can learn to love themselves the way they are. I love to see heavy women who are funny, good dancers, and enjoy eating. I believe people can learn to love their bodies no matter what society's norms appear to be.

I love to look at people who are naked. Going to the baths at Esalen where clothing is optional ministers to my voyeuristic needs. I can look and not touch. I think I'd like to be in a nudist colony. The truth is that I am so used to being clothed, I'd be uncomfortable without clothes. Chilly too. But I still like to look.

I thank God for my body. It is a gift to me. I did not earn it. I was given a good face. "Monday's child is fair of face" goes the old rhyme. I was born on a Monday. I learned that I was attractive, especially to women. That is what has helped make me secure and confident.

I am six feet, four inches tall. Always the tallest, I was last in line when we had to line up in size place when I was in grammar school. Being tall helped me as an athlete. My size helped me enjoy football, baseball, basketball, swimming, and even some tennis.

Yet my internal body is a mystery to me. The beat of my heart goes on without my paying any attention. A moderate diet should keep the arteries doing what they should. The system that moves food through my body works fairly well except for when I eat and drink too much. The blood circulates. The nerves snap along. All are pretty mysterious to me. I remember the late Bob Colton, MD, said it takes about two years to really learn how the body works.

I worry that there will be pain before I die. There probably will be, but I hope not.

CHAPTER 3

BRAIN MASSAGE

I write to keep my brain massaged. Thinking, imagining, and finding a point of view give an agile toggle to my brain and keep it moving. My theory is that the more I use my brain, the more it will repair itself and prolong its power. I have abused my physical brain by banging it around in violent football and basketball in my youth, and by drinking alcohol. Stress, lying, and making excuses for my behavior have damaged my brain. I have no scientific evidence that this is true, yet common sense tells me so.

My mind is dependent on my brain. Thinking and imagination are the results of brainpower. My mind makes me love and appreciate food, art, and good writing. The mix of brain and mind is a whole field of study. Science keeps determining the connections and helps people continue to keep healthy brains and good minds.

When I retired in 2002, I decided to write five hundred words every day to keep my brain/mind as healthy as possible. I have done pretty well. I write letters to the editor, open forum pieces, and lots of letters and emails. I keep a journal. I have written *Memoir RWC*. Short essays and opinion pieces have been collected into my *Essays Irreverent*. One of my most favorite writing exercises is to write a daughter letter each Saturday. It goes to Leigh Cromey and Sarah and

Jessica Buck (Sarah and Jessica married the Buck brothers) and now I include my grandchildren, Catherine and Daniel Lindsay, and Mary Charlotte, Eric, and Caleb Buck. I sometimes include my brother Edwin and his wife Pamela, as well as my two first cousins, Richard Reinemann and Phyllis Thanner, as well as their spouses, Charlotte Reinemann and Joe Thanner.

I would like to include Ann's family but she prefers I not. She fears my radical political and sex ideas would not be received well by her more conservative Mormon family. I honor her wishes in the matter. However, I think she underestimates their tolerance and openness. My personal experience of them makes me think they will read what they want and just think I am a typical left wing, knee-jerk, liberal Democrat Episcopalian. I think Ann believes my ideas will reflect badly on her and her family members won't love and respect her any more. I think they love and respect me just fine knowing how different our views are on religion and politics.

I also have a blog, Cromey.blogspot.com. On it I have over 400 entries, which I have written since it began shortly after I retired. In addition, I send out opinion pieces about church and/or state to 500 mostly clergy on my mailing list.

I often wonder how many people read my blog or my opinion pieces. My job is to write them and send them out. Their job is to read them or not and use them as they can. I get some feedback from these emailings but not a lot. In some ways, it is like preaching. I say the words, and I have no idea how much the listeners have heard, what they think about it, or do about what I suggest. I guess the writing works on me. I hope it works for some of my readers or listeners.

My hope is that my writing, which I enjoy, doing, helps keep my brain healthy and my mind active. Of course, I am afraid of dementia and Alzheimer's. I note I have some memory loss like forgetting people's names and the names of fruits and vegetables or of places I used to know well. So far, Ann has not complained.

I enjoy reading and spend at least an hour a day on books. I love mysteries, literary novels, biographies, history, and Biblical and theological studies. I also read the San Francisco Chronicle and the N.Y. Times abridged version on line, plus the Sunday New York Times.

Looking on the net, I found some interesting stuff on aging. There is a lot on how the brain works, how it shrinks and deteriorates. At this stage of my life I want to know what things may help prevent further deterioration and might even improve my brain functioning.

A lifetime of reading, learning, conversation and even games like chess keep the mind vigorous and active. I am not so sure that constantly watching Television and the commercials contribute much to brainpower. Some think Alzheimer disease is warded off by vigorous brain use.

A FaceBook post read:

Leo Tolstoy learned to ride a bicycle at 67

Queen Victoria began learning Hindustani at 68

Giuseppe Verdi was still composing operas in his 80s

Somerset Maugham wrote his last book at 84

Frank Lloyd Wright designed his last building at 89

In their 90s, Robert Frost was writing poems and George Bernard Shaw was writing plays, Georgia O'Keefe was painting pictures, and Pablo Casals was playing cello

Oliver Wendell Holmes was still dominating the Supreme Court until he retired at 91

Linus Pauling was actively publishing just before his death at age 93.

Leopold Stokowski recorded 20 albums in his 90s and signed a six-year contract at 96.

Here are morsels on enjoying aging. Controlling blood cholesterol is aided by losing weight and regular exercise and physical activity. Eating plenty of fruits and vegetables. These common sense activities help keep our brains healthy

Engaging in intellectually stimulating activities and maintaining close social ties with family, friends, and community help keep our brains healthy. I get my community from church and a wide variety of friendships and a regular correspondence with my family and many friends.

Good advice about aging abounds. Many magazines carry articles about it. The American Association of Retired People (AARP) magazine has articles to help. Health newsletters from Harvard, Yale, Stanford, and other places provide valuable and concrete information. I read the stuff and pick and choose what is helpful and relates to me.

CHAPTER 4

GEEZER SEX

A television crew asked a 107-year-old man what was the secret of his longevity.

"It's because I gave up sex," he said.

"When did you give up sex?" asked the reporter.

"Fifteen years ago."

"I see," said the reporter. "And why did you give up sex?"

"I had to. I like older women."

I am the geezer. One look at Ann and you know she is not a geezer. I show my age more than she does. I am retired and 86 years old at this writing. I have been retired for 15 years. Like a teen boy I think of sex all the time. Advertising in newspapers, television, and movie plots keep sex before my eyes. I would rather see sex scenes than violent ones on TV and in movies. All this in addition to my own personal sexual thoughts and feelings keep sex on my mind and I'll bet on other people's minds but they won't admit it. Well I admit it and enjoy my sexuality.

Statistics indicate older Americans are interested in their sexuality. The drive does not diminish necessarily with aging. Many people have little or no sex when reaching 70. They should not be surprised to find they have poor sex as they become older. So, one can expect good sex when we get older even if we have been having good sex all along.

It is certainly true that as our bodies age, our sexual capacities diminish, but certainly do not disappear. Many women's vagina walls may become dry and tender. Lubricants can help. Men's erections may be softer than they were when younger. Viagra and Cialis and other pills and treatments help many men achieve better erections. Orgasms may be less deep and powerful.

Good sex at any age depends on good communication. Young people often have sex problems because they are not confident enough to speak about what they like or don't like about having intercourse. "You are touching my breasts too hard." "I want us to kiss longer." "I want you to touch my penis." Learning to communicate clearly about our sexual needs can only improve our enjoyment of sex.

Younger and older people can have warm delicious conversation about how often they should have intercourse. Specific talk about oral sex can be embarrassing and fun too.

Older men can learn to laugh when their penises look and feel like marshmallows. Women can talk about how nice it is to just lie there and let the man do the work. Laugh when the orgasm feels more like a sneeze or a squirt than any great thrill.

Sex and intimacy and just holding and cuddling are the glue that keeps a relationship warm. One older couple I know has a warm relationship. He has had surgery so that he cannot have an erection. I can only imagine the possible variations so that both are pleased and pleasured. The man can help bring the woman to orgasm by oral sex, licking and kissing her clitoris and vaginal area. The man can receive pleasure when he knows his partner is pleasured. The woman with her hands and tongue and mouth may caress the man's genitalia and evoke intimacy. In fact many men who can't have erections can still have orgasms. Cuddling, massage and bathing together can bring love and intimacy.

With good communication comes trust. Couples can try new and unusual ways to have sex and closeness if they trust each other.

Good sex is quite available for people of all ages and especially for the elderly.

We found many ways to arouse ourselves. We share our sexual fantasies and dreams. We talk about our past sexual experiences. Ann does not want me to talk about previous loves and sexual partners. We share our dreams almost every day, especially if they have sexual content. Our motto is if we don't want to share the dream, then we have to do it. It is always fun and sometimes arousing.

Geezer Sex

Ann and I often talked and read about sex. She and I sat down one day and came up with ideas and topics for Geezer Sex. The list is also of interest to anyone interested in sex.

Sex is good for your health. It is a good way to convey the love we have for one another. It increases our intimacy. The physical exertion for an active man exerts the heart and breathing. The physical pleasure of orgasm relaxes and calms the body. Pillow talk after sex increases intimacy and physical closeness.

Love and laugh at being a Geezer who wants sex. I am good at laughing at myself. As my sexual prowess began to diminish, I made fun of myself. When my penis got soft I would brag that my penis now resembled a wet noodle. I laughed and cried, "Oh how I miss the old days." With Ann, I could share and laugh about my limitations. "What's the matter," she'd ask, "Can't get it up?" I would grimace with horror and then laugh.

We had favorite positions that I can't do any more. My aging and aching body can't squirm, kneel, or change positions easily. It is one more item worth chuckling about and even regretting a bit. We talk about it and it doesn't matter much.

In my 70s I began to use Viagra to get and keep an erection. The pill made my nose get stuffed. I switched to Cialis, which worked fine for a long time. Later Dr. Gary Feldman suggested I use ½ Cialis the night before sex and one in the morning. That worked for a while and then I took a half at night, later a whole one at night and then two in the morning. Dr. Anna Beyer, my cardiologist, said there is not a cardiovascular danger using sexual dysfunctional pills.

Frequency is another issue for geezer sex. Ann and I used to make love three times a day when we first lived together and then married. I was in my early 50s and Ann was in her 40s. We got down to once a day, every day. Then every other day, three times a week, and then once a week. And then not-so-much. I am 86 and Ann is 75.

Vaginal lube for Ann became a concern for Ann when she was in her 60s. Thinning vaginal walls made intercourse irritating and painful. She experimented with a variety of lubes and settled on Just Between Us from Key West Aloe, a Florida firm.

What will the children think, or the neighbors, when they discover we are having intercourse? Sometimes Ann and I are noisy in our lovemaking. This is a concern when we stay in other people's homes. The son of one of Ann's teacher friends coined the term geezer sex. This friend reported that when her teen son realized his divorced mother was having sex with her "boyfriend," he gasped, "Oooooweeeegeezer sex."

One of my daughters lived with us for a year when she was in her twenties. She told her sisters, "I know it'll be over soon when the floor stops creaking."

If it doesn't come naturally, learn to be affectionate. Much kissing, hugging, petting, touching, caressing literally keeps us in touch with each other but helps keeps us aroused and physically aware. Ann and I are in constant physical touch with each other. I feel sad when we are with other couples who seldom even touch each other.

I have found over the years that I accept my body as it is. Growing older, my skin is flabby and wrinkled. I appear tall, although Ann has to remind me to stand up straight a lot. I admit to a jot of pleasure when people are surprised that I am 86.

Ann's body always gives me pleasure to look at and to touch, kiss and caress. We often talk about our bodies and what we appreciate about each other's body. Ann is very careful about her diet and weight. She walks and exercises a lot. We are both delighted when people remark that she looks so much younger than her age.

I led a therapy group once where a young Asian man spoke of how he hated his body. Much of his chest and neck were badly scarred after he was caught in a fire. After he talked about his pain, I asked him to take his shirt off and let us see the scarring. Reluctantly he did so. I asked his permission to look at and touch the scars. He allowed other members of the group to touch the scars. Yes, the scars felt taut and were uneven. Yet everyone in the group told him that while the scars were not pretty, he was a good person and a worthwhile human being. He wept with a sad joy and began to feel better about his body and himself.

Sex is better, more fun and arousing if we talk freely about cock sucking and pussy licking. Anal sex—love it or leave it. Some women like it or at least are willing to do it. Some men like to have anal intercourse with other men. Couples should have a frank talk about what they want or do not want about anal intercourse. There is nothing bad, wrong or evil about it. It is a matter of personal choice and interest. Just talking about it lessens the tension couples have about it.

Well, it is time to own up to the fact that my cock isn't going to get very hard now that I have reached 86 plus. I have even tried Muse. It is a thin plastic tube that goes down my penis and then a small amount of some chemical is injected into the depths of my urethra. After ten minutes my cock gets hard enough, sometimes, to fuck Ann. She is enormously patient with my sexual shenanigans, hard, soft, floppy, and sometimes solid for mutual orgasm. I do hope this will change but I am realistic and so is Ann.

This is the end of having erections hard enough to satisfy me and even go into Ann's sweet body. My first worry is that Ann will miss straight fucking, yearn for it, and will find another man to fuck her. She reassures me over and over again that she is and will be faithful to me. I am mostly satisfied with her pledges but I still worry a bit that temptation may wend her way to a sex contact with another man. She certainly is attractive enough and sexy enough to seduce or even be seduced. She seduces me all the time and I can't do anything about it.

I notice I don't miss the sexual activity too much, although I do think about fucking Ann a lot. I think about the old days with her, and other women before our marriage. I do enjoy some of the free porn on the Internet but it is best for seeing lovely women naked and sexually aroused. The men usually look and act like brutes or nerds.

I suspect I will gently ease out of this sexual anxiety and be at peace with little or no sexual performance. I feel sad writing those words. Good sex has been such a wonderful part of my life and our lives as a married couple.

Certainly my sex drive, among other things, ruined my first marriage to Lillian, and the divorce hurt my daughters. Nevertheless, sex has always been wonderful, exciting, orgasmic, sensual, powerful, pleasurable, relaxing, and visceral. Sex has driven me to love my body and women's bodies. I have never had sexual feelings toward men, nor desire for personal or sexual intimacy with them. I rejoice that same-gender lovers enjoy sex and deep love.

I have had sex with many women. I have lost count actually. However, I have not had sex with another woman in the 34 years Ann and I have been married. I like women, looking at them, wishing I could see then naked, and want to touch some women's breasts. I have not touched anyone. Some years ago, I was at Esalen Institute at the communal baths and did enjoy looking at the naked women climbing in and out of the hot tubs and taking showers in the washhouse overlooking the Pacific Ocean. I like looking at women's breasts and nakedness when I see them (rarely) in magazine photos.

My mind has sex urges all the time. I enjoy them and don't want them ever to go away. Ann often shows me her lovely naked body, PTA—pussy tits and ass—as we like to say. Into her nightie, or the shower, she often pauses to let me admire her body. Sex is always in the air and my mind. I just can't get my cock erect much anymore.

I have always loved feeling Ann up. She says she likes it. I stand behind her and put my hands around her breasts and gently jostle them. She pushes her ass into my crotch. Ann kisses me on the forehead when she leaves the room or even when she re-enters. She often puts her hand on my crotch and it always feels good, sexy, but it no longer causes an erection. Sometimes I pretend to blame her because she can't arouse me anymore and we both chuckle. Orgasm for me when I masturbate feels just a little better than a sneeze.

We have always been very affectionate with one another. We both enjoy embracing and being embraced, kissing, and being kissed. I have to remind Ann and myself that we must cuddle naked in bed, body-to-body, lips-to-lips, and sex kisses more often, especially since I can't get erect enough to fuck. I do love just being close, kissing and fondling.

Regular sexual and physical closeness is a sacrament of our love for each other.

CHAPTER 5

WE DIE NOT PASS AWAY

Long before I retired I thought a lot about death. I asked a friend about why I am thinking so much about death. She wisely pointed out that in those years 1989-94, I was pastor to dying young men who had HIV disease. At Trinity during those years we conducted funerals for 75 men between 25-35 who had contracted AIDS. Death was in front of me every day.

Her remarks put my thinking about death in some perspective. Yet I still thought about death a lot. I wrote about it my journal. The thoughts did not interfere with my work or love life. In fact, I rather enjoyed thinking about death and dying.

I became intrigued with the funeral business after I was ordained. I became rector of the Church of the Holy Nativity in the Bronx, New York. Lyle Knittel was the church funeral director. Not many churches have such a person, but Lyle had been there long before I came. Many members, not all, used his services to remove, prepare, and bury the dead family members and friends of our parish. Many times, we conducted funerals together.

Jessica Mitford's book *The American Way of Death* was published in the 1950s. It was an expose of funeral practices that often bilked the grieving into spending vast amounts of money on needless funeral services. Lyle of course was offended but I thought Mitford was right.

British author Evelyn Waugh took a swipe at American sentimentalism in his book *The Loved One*. I found his views hilarious and worthwhile.

I also read the works of Thomas Lynch, Funeral Director and poet. *The Undertaking: Life Studies from the Dismal Trade* is a wonderful look at death and funerals. He is funny yet serious about taking death with careful consideration.

I once told Richard Turley, my parish administrator at Trinity, never to use the words passed away, departed, fell asleep, or any other such abomination in mailings from the church. When you die, you die.

I adhere to the usual clichés. I am not afraid of dying but I do fear suffering. Put me out of my misery. Ann and I have signed the usual papers to allow doctors to let me die if there is no hope of a decent life. I am more than happy to have a doctor rid me of misery even if he or she does something illegal. I also believe that all of us should have the legal right to an assisted suicide.

As a lifelong Christian I believe there is life after death. As a lifelong product of the scientific and logical positivist world, I have no concrete evidence that there is life after death. I like the *Book of Common Prayer* notion that there is "a sure and certain hope" in a resurrection and new life after death. I hope there is. Wouldn't it be fun to see my dad and mom again?

I have visited Sullivan's Funeral Home on Market Street in San Francisco. I told Mr. Sullivan the funeral director of my wishes. When I die, I want my body taken to the funeral home and refrigerated, not embalmed. If my daughters and brother wish to journey to San Francisco from the East Coast to attend the funeral, the funeral will be held within a week or so of my death.

My body will be placed in an inexpensive wooden casket. At the funeral, the casket will be taken to St. John's Church, San Francisco. There a pall will be placed over the casket, and the casket will be taken into the nave of the church. There will be a full choral liturgy, with incense and hymns chosen by me. The preacher will be the present Vicar of St. John's. If he is not available, my wife Ann will choose the preacher. My body is to be cremated and the ashes scattered in the garden at St. John's.

So many people are so frightened of death they cannot even make a will. I for one try to look at my death seriously. Making a will and a plan for the funeral and disposal of my body makes me more comfortable with my death. I think it is also a responsible thing to do so my family and friends are not burdened with that chore.

I just read Autil Gawande's book *Being Mortal*. He raises important issues about the end of life choices. He wants us to live the last years with dignity and autonomy, not in warehouses for the aged infirm.

He points out several facilities for the aging, which focus on privacy, self-determination, loose feeding schedules, and consultation with staff and doctors about measures to be taken for safety.

For doctors, he points out that there is a time to fix or not. He uses his own father as an example. He had a spinal cord tumor. They decided not to fix the tumor, which might have made him a paraplegic. They decided to do nothing and his father lived four more years and could perform surgery and practice medicine.

He provides important questions to be discussed with spouse, family, and doctors.

1. Do you want to be resuscitated if your heart stops?

2. Do you want aggressive treatment such as intubation or mechanical ventilation?

3. Do you want antibiotics?

4. Do you want tube or intravenous feeding if you can't eat on your own?

It is important that each of us face the reality of sickness and death.

Talking about the issues, just verbalizing the fears and concerns can make one more comfortable facing the issues.

I remember one parishioner who was so fearful, he could not make a will or even a letter saying what he wanted for a funeral, burial, or disposing of his clothes and books.

Reading Dr. Gawande's book made me think about what happens if I get seriously ill. I want to stay at home as long as possible. I do not want to die in a hospital or nursing home unless it is absolutely necessary. There are a number of programs, even public ones that provide help to a patient who is incapacitated to live at home. The "Village" program is one such. Visiting nurses, visiting hospice care, family and friends can be called upon to help Ann or me, whoever is the caregiver. We cannot be afraid to ask for help. People yearn to help others.

Many people do not want funerals after they die. They or their families plan to have a celebration of the deceased's life. Ann and I went to one recently. The event was held in a beautiful suburban home. The guests gathered for wine and cheese. Soon the group was called together and we sat in folding chairs under the trees and a tent. The daughter of the deceased gave a long clever, funny, and poignant speech about her enormously talented father. Then many individuals stood and spoke of how Larry had influenced and affected their lives. It was a fine event.

The trouble with such events is that there is seldom mention of death, grief, sadness, or mourning. A good church funeral is a service of worship of God. It is a thanksgiving for the gift of life, and an opportunity to weep and mourn benefitting the family but also for the relatives and friends of the deceased.

With fewer people identifying with a religious heritage, substitute ceremonies like celebrations of life become the norm.

CHAPTER 6

ANN

What a wonderful wife I have. She is patient with my foibles. She smiles when I fume about the stupidity of the church dragging its feet about peace. She gives me positive and negative feedback about my preaching. She catches me being abstract, suggesting I use an illustration or tell a story. If I mention love, she'll say, "Give an example." Her responses are always positive, helpful.

Before we entered into holy matrimony, Ann and I had a kind of pre-nup agreement.

We adopted the late George Leonard's term "High Monogamy." We agreed to no fucking around. We chose full faithful monogamy as a basic tenet of our marriage. If either of us were attracted to another man or woman we would talk about those feelings with each other. When Ann came home from work, I would ask, "Were you sexually attracted to any one today, dear?" She would ask the same question of me. Both of us had sexual feelings toward others from time to time. We shared those feelings with each other. I was, and still am, very jealous and Ann is too. Those loaded questions became part of our life together. Those conversations lightened our jealousy. They blew the charge of sexual feelings toward others. I did not have to hold on to secrets.

I found that if I did not want to talk about or reveal something that was exactly what I needed to talk about.

We chose to tell each other the truth and not hold back any secrets. If I dreamed or fantasized of having sex with another woman, I would tell Ann. She did the same for me. Those revelations made for delicious breakfast conversations.

I learned about the importance of telling the truth, self-revelation, and clear communication from my time at Esalen Institute in the Residential Fellow program led by Will Schutz in 1968. I learned much from the writing and groups led by Gerald Walker Smith and in the EST seminars led by Werner Erhard.

When Ann and I married in 1983, I was 52 and Ann was 41. We had both been married before and had suffered through divorce. As Beth Gutcheon says, "You had trial marriages." We had learned plenty and were able to make such agreements about sexual behavior. It is hard for young marrieds to do so. They have not had so much life experience.

Not long after I retired, I needed left knee replacement surgery. There were complications. I spent some time in the hospital and recovering at home. Ann was so patient and helpful as I was mostly helpless for a week or so. She visited twice a day in the hospital. After I recovered from that, I had surgery on a melanoma on my back. As that healed I had a minor stroke, which healed quickly with no perceivable damage. Then in the fall of 2016, I got a bout of pneumonia, which took two weeks to repair.

Ann was there taking care of me, shopping and cooking and doing the dishes. One day she was in Safeway in the evening. She ran into Burton Weaver, former organist at Trinity, who directed her to the items she needed. He told me that she looked like a lost soul wandering around the market. She seldom goes shopping as I do all the shopping and cooking. She is a superb cook but loves it that I take care of that part of our lives. I enjoy it very much. I am a fine housewife.

She has travelled to Vietnam, Brazil, Bhutan, and Patagonia since she retired. While delighted to alleviate her travel lust, she is very anxious about leaving me home alone while she is away for three weeks. I constantly reassure her that it is fine for her to go. I have daughters in New England and friends in Palm Springs whom I love to visit. I also love to be at home alone in our comfortable flat in San Francisco. While away, Ann calls me almost every day to keep in touch and tell me that she adores me. I like that.

Ann always dresses with great care and always looks wonderful. She takes classes at the Fromm Institute, goes to book groups, walks, and talks with her friends. She always wears perfectly matched or contrasting colorful outfits. She wears lots of sunblock to protect her smooth fair skin.

She loves to dress up when we go to church on Sundays and when she goes to the opera and symphony. (I am on parole from the latter two.) She has a collection of vintage dresses and suits as well as carefully chosen garments of her own. Colors range from blues, to reds and turquoise. She is famous for her hats, large and small, veiled and open faced, wide brimmed and no brim in every conceivable color and even a feather or two.

Ann reads constantly and at present is in four book groups. One of her groups consists of three women who had been Ann's students when they were in high school. They asked Ann to be in the group. She had inspired them to read and travel. I admire her willingness to read many books that were chosen by the groups and not necessarily ones she likes much. She is writing a book entitled *Vagabond Virgins* about travelling and hitchhiking in Europe, North Africa, and the Middle East with her younger sister. She works regularly on the book and gets advice from her friends and a writing group.

Ann is interested in almost everything. The stars, the moon, interstellar space, flowers, birds, animals, and all things in nature hold her in thrall. She loves to be out in nature. Walking trails with an ocean view and bird watching delight her. She likes hiking in the Wasatch Mountains when we stay at our cabin in Utah each summer. She loves museums; the Met in New York City is her favorite. She'd rent rooms inside if it were allowed. She loves paintings, sculpture, fine cloth, and jewelry. The Greeks, Romans, and Egyptians especially move her.

Things mechanical hold no interest for her. Touring a factory or a railroad museum, or examining the internal life of a car, are regarded as torture. She loves music and attends the symphony and opera every season.

Ann and I have always been very sexual. Even in our early retirement we had intercourse twice a week. I have been using Cialis since I was in my 70s. Even with a variety of pills and regular delightful foreplay and lots of discussion, my penis just slowly became less able to stay erect enough to be pleasing to either of us. We call him the marshmallow these days. When in the right mood we have oral sex, going down on each other. We both love doing that. We have talked about it and gently agreed to stick with regular cuddling and I hope for "old days" to come again.

Since Ann is 11 years younger than I, my biggest fear is that she would want a younger and more sexually stimulating man than I am these days. She assures and re-assures me that she is not interested in other men and does not yearn for intercourse like we both did earlier in our relationship. I really do believe her and there has been no indication that she wants other men.

We married in 1983 and had a vigorous social life. We entertained friends and our families with dinner parties with drinks, wine, dinners, and desserts. While I was rector, we were invited out to dinner three times a month. Sometimes we ate out three times on a weekend. When I retired in 2002, our somewhat lavish entertainments began to diminish. We both were glad of it. In the last few years we have enjoyed entertaining at home by inviting guests and ordering take-out Indian, Vietnamese, or Thai food. With no shopping or cooking and just a bit of cleanup, entertaining is much easier. Ann is wonderful as she does most of the plating and cleanup.

Ann thinks I am funny. She inevitably laughs at my jokes, one liners puns and even when I show her cartoons in magazines and the newspaper. I sometimes wonder how she puts up with me. We both are very affectionate with one another. Whenever Ann comes into a room where I am she almost always kisses me on the forehead and does the same when she leaves before me. I enjoy her constant affection and attention.

Ann is 5'4" tall and weighs 120 lbs. She weighs herself daily to make sure she doesn't blossom too much. Her dark blue eyes emerge from her flawless complexion. Her hair is a blond gray. She changes hairstyles regularly. She says she always hates her hair when she returns from the stylist. In a day or two she does not mention it again. Her hair always looks lovely to me. She stands up straight with shoulders back. Her body is sturdy and strong, reflecting the exercises she does each day. I admire her persistence. Her breasts are firm and just the right size to fit into my hands. Her pussy hair is dark, curly and fetching to look at and touch. When she takes off her clothes to enter the shower or put on her nightie, she often will whistle and say "Nakies." My little daughters used to say that when they were nude. I love to look at Ann's lovely naked body and she often shows herself off to me.

Ann is very smart. With high intelligence and hard work, she got top grades in high school, college, and graduate school. She holds a master's degree in English. She always taught high school English in girls Catholic Schools and was English Department Head for thirty-three years. She loved her work with her students.

Growing up a Mormon in Salt Lake City, Utah, she rebelled against that religion when she was in her 20s. She practiced no religion until we met in the early 1980s. She hiked on weekends and enjoyed the mysticism of nature. When we became serious about each other, I was already the rector of Trinity. She chose to give up hiking and come to church to hear me preach. She found she liked the ritual, beauty, music, and pageantry of the Episcopal Church and after a while became a member. After we retired we have continued to go to church together. We are not particularly pious, but we do say a prayer blessing the food and those who are hungry and who need healing.

Ann is an accumulator. We have shelves piled with textiles, boxes of items of art from her extensive world travels, and closets full of vintage clothes that Ann loves and hates to throw or give away. We have the one in, one out rule, which sometimes gets honored. I love to buy books and often don't give one away when I purchase a new one. Over the years, I have grown to not care so much about the collections. Many of the items are quite beautiful. Ann hates to throw away leftovers. I have taken the courageous step of tossing fridge items that begin to grow cotton.

We both are neatniks so our flat is always easy to look at and delightful to gaze upon. We both know automatically when it is time to toss stuff.

We have had cleaning help. Neither of us likes to vacuum, dust, or change the bed. Our cleaning "lady" usually comes from Mexico or South America. Ann is always so nice to the women and has enough Spanish to get simple instructions across. Rosy, our present helper, has a little girl who loves school and art. Ann gives presents, clothes, and sometimes food for Yancy. I am so happy that Ann is generous and humane with our helpers.

Ann loves the newspapers. She reads the San Francisco Chronicle every day and the New York Times Sunday edition every week. She reads the newspapers very slowly and carefully, often making her late for her next scheduled activity. She is convinced that is it is a genetic trait as her sister Beau is the same way. In addition, she reads The New Yorker slowly and they pile up for months until in exasperation she gives them to our tenants. I am a fast reader and get through the material quickly. Either way, neither of us can remember much of all we have read. Neither of us watches TV news. Ann watches very selective programs on KQED. I like to watch DVDs or streaming videos.

Ann is a very patient and careful person. She is a wonderfully safe driver. Nowadays she does all the driving when we go out together and especially at night. I have full confidence in her driving. She is a careful decision maker. I often have to hustle her along a bit as I am a very impatient man. When she makes a decision, it is almost always the correct one. I feel very safe in her hands.

I love and adore my Ann. I cannot conceive of living long should she pre-decease me. I think of her warmly and with delight all through the day. I love to listen to her stories and enjoy the pleasure she has in relating them. I love being her wife and her husband. It gives me great delight to dine with her at our breakfasts and dinners. I appreciate her enthusiasm for our life together for me. Her constant kisses and touches make me love her all the more. I use these old words to express how I feel about Ann, "With my body, I thee worship."

CHAPTER 7

MORE MONEY

We have more money in retirement than we had while working. We went to Laurie Nardone, a financial Planner, recommended by Sue Dunlap, a close friend. Laurie looked over our financial situation. It consists of my pension from the Church Pension Fund of the Episcopal Church, and Social Security payments earned by Ann and me over the years we worked. In addition, Ann has income from a 403(b) through TIAA-CREF and another investment.

We own a three-flat building in San Francisco. We live in one flat and rent out the other two. The income from the rented flats pays our mortgage, insurance, and taxes. We essentially live rent-free. We also own a building in Salt Lake City. Ann was raised there and most of her family lives in the city. The Salt Lake City rent pays for the mortgage and taxes. It might be a retirement home for us.

After looking over our financial situation Laurie told us we were not spending enough money. Like many of us older people from Depression era parents we lived frugally and were not aware of the value of our assets. In any case, we spend more money now than we ever did before. We have enough assets that we do not have to worry about running out of money.

Not every retired person is in our financial situation. We

are happy with our newfound prosperity. I worked as a cleric for most of my working life. For 11 years, I worked as a private Marriage and Family Therapist. My highest income year was the year before my retirement. It was $75,000. Ann worked for over thirty years as a high school English teacher. Her highest salary was $83,000.

I have adjusted easily to spending more money. I think of my spending as buying toys. I enjoy my computer, printer, cell phone, and tablet. I bought a Bose audio system for my study. Our kitchen and living room audio systems are over thirty years old. We don't plan to replace them until we have to. We have one television set that can show DVDs. We seldom watch TV. I like to watch Netflix shows on my computer, which lets Ann read undisturbed.

We travel some together. We sailed the Queen Mary round trip and spent a month in London in 2013. We spend two weeks each summer in our cabin in Brighton, Utah. The last three years we have spent Thanksgiving in New England at the homes of my daughters Leigh, Sarah, and Jessica and their families. After that we spent time in Manhattan visiting old friends and museums. We will again go to Puerto Vallarta this winter for two weeks. Ann has travelled without me to Bhutan and Patagonia.

Ann and I give each other freedom to do what we want either together or apart. This has hardly changed at all since we retired. Ann loves the symphony and the opera. I do not. She goes to those events on her own or with friends. I enjoy staying home, reading, and watching Netflix shows. I feel a little guilty when Ann goes out unaccompanied but not too much. She seems fine about doing what she wants to do. These days the cost of the major cultural events is not a matter of concern.

The sense of freedom that our prosperity brings is wonderful. We are not big spenders anyway. My VW New Beetle is vintage 2002. Ann bought a new Honda in 2016 for cash. We don't desire a boat, a plane, or another home in the country. We spend on food, booze, wine, and entertaining. We have some housecleaning help. We are grateful for our financial wellbeing and only hope more retired people can be as fortunate as we are.

More thoughts on money

Why am I still anxious about money? We have plenty, there is little chance we will go broke. I find myself anxious if we make large expenditures for travel. I am not anxious enough to stop spending money on Ann's or my travel expense. It is a niggling, internal fear that I won't have enough. When our checking account balance gets below $10,000, I get nervous. Don't laugh, but it is true. If we have to sell some stock to catch up on bills I feel bad.

Yet when I have some cash I want to tip generously. I got my brown shoes shined yesterday for $25. I gave the man two twenties and asked him to keep the change. I bought a $6.50 hot dog and gave the man a ten and told him to keep the change. I like over tipping. Laura-Lee, my hair cutter, charges $27.00 for a haircut, I give her forty. I am generous when I get a mani-pedi; I tip on how many women wait on me. I tip 20-25% at restaurants. But these are small amounts. Tipping generously makes me feel good. It helps low income people have a bit more.

I can't help my being judgmental when I read how much money people have. I know this has always been true. Many people accumulate vast amounts of money, property, and gadgets. Money brings power. I wonder if I had more money would I feel more powerful?

Great wealth helps create great art, music, and sculpture. Churches, cathedrals, and fine buildings need huge amounts of money to be built.

Is it moral to make art and build buildings while so many people are poor? Yes, great art is supposed to uplift and inspire people. The poor seldom see great art much less great buildings.

It must be greed that makes good people want to pay low wages. Profits are made by cutting costs and lowering wages and firing employees.

Of course, if the companies paid employees money enough to buy insurance, have sick leave, and live well, then I'd have no beef. However, the whole capitalist system creates wealth and profits for the rich, some for the middle class, and the crumbs for the rest.

CHAPTER 8

MY CHILDREN

Leigh

Daughter Leigh was born in 1956. She was the first child. A tall child, she was not only the first-born but also the longest. Much taller than her sisters and ordered them around until they toughened and asserted themselves.

She went to Gettysburg College in Pennsylvania.

She was very sad at the divorce. She received some therapy and has worked through her sadness and anger.

Her plan was to marry, have babies and be a housewife. Before that she got a Master's degree in University Administration. She is smart, quite pretty, and had no trouble meeting men. She married a reluctant David Lindsay and had two boys and then Catherine.

Austin her first-born died at 22 from a drug overdose. Leigh was devastated. She took a long time to recover. She has a fine job as an administrator at the Yale University Medical School herding around the first-year medical students. She and David divorced and she took her maiden name. She has a new sweetie, Rich. They are happy together, with no immediate plans to marry.

Leigh is strong, witty, and independent minded. She is thinking about retirement already. Daniel has not finished college and is under-employed living in Portland, OR. Catherine is a junior at University of Connecticut.

Sarah

Sarah was born in 1958. She is the clever operator. She would say, "Dad, are you free after dinner?" "OK, take us to Baskin-Robbins for ice cream." She set me up for a positive answer. I saw her at a grammar school parent's night demonstration. Sarah worked with deliberation and speed on her project.

Later when she was in college she decided to become a nurse. She had trouble with Physics so she went out and hired a tutor all on her own. She completed her nurses training, got a Master of Science degree, and has worked at Massachusetts General Hospital in Boston as a pediatric critical care nurse.

She is of middle height, gray brown hair, hazel eyes and wears no make-up. She had a boy and a girl with Greg Buck. She divorced him and lives happily in Andover, MA with Greg Bird her beloved man. Mary-Charlotte and Eric have finished college and are working.

Sarah is active in her parish, Christ Church, Andover, MA. She has many women friends and they socialize and travel to warm weather in winter.

Jessica

Some pictures of her show her grumpy. Others depict the clown. After Lillian's and my divorce, one time when she was eleven, she flew from Boston to San Francisco all by herself to meet me. She got off the plane carrying a doll. Jess, as we kissed and hugged, was cool, unruffled, and independent.

She was an exchange student in Israel for a summer and then went back for a whole year staying with an Israeli family. Here was this tall skinny blond shiksa adored by the children of the family. She finished college, got a Master's in School Counseling. She married Greg's brother Ben Buck and their son Caleb is in the working world.

Jessica was a counselor in a middle school in Connecticut. When students get angry and violent, she knows how to take them down to prevent them hurting themselves or others. She recently retired from the school and now has a private counseling practice in Litchfield, CT.

Jessica is blond, has long curled hair, lots of make-up, loves clothes, and is quite glamorous.

All three

My three daughters Leigh, Sarah, and Jessica have been married, had children, and two are divorced. They are all employed, enjoy their work, and are close to their children. Leigh and Sarah, both divorced, have delightful men in their lives. Neither they nor I push for marriage. The "girls" are all in their fifties, adult, mature, and intelligent women. It is none of my business about how they live their personal lives.

Since my daughters grew up in New England in Lillian's home, I have treated them as mature young women. On my trips to visit them, we dined out, went to museums, went bowling, to the movies and visited with their friends and their families. One of the parents even invited me to Thanksgiving Dinner at their home. The daughter-visits in the summers of the 1970s were fun and the girls did all the delightful San Francisco activities. They almost always invited a girl friend to come along.

We have always enjoyed each other's company. After I retired in 2002, Ann and I visited the daughters in their homes. Leigh, Sarah, and Jessica came to San Francisco to celebrate my 80th birthday.

We have started a tradition of Ann and I having Thanksgiving Dinner at the homes of one of my daughters. Sarah had the first one, Jessica the second, and then Leigh in 2015. Ann and I would then spend a few days in Manhattan seeing the museums and friends.

These TG dinners occurred after Lillian's death, June 9, 2009. She and the daughters and others had had TG dinners. We dined with our friends.

Neither Ann nor I are very judgmental about my daughters'

personal lives. They are mature adults and quite capable of making decision without input or approval from us. Leigh did come to San Francisco to chat with us when she decided she wanted to divorce David. I felt honored and flattered that she came to talk with us about her situation.

My daughters always invited us to stay in their homes when we visited. We don't do that anymore. We prefer the privacy and freedom of staying at a nearby hotel. However, that means someone in the family must transport us back and forth from hotel to the appropriate home. Now that the grandchildren all drive the burden is light.

I feel so moved and sad that Leigh had such a wretched decade. David battled every day and word of the divorce settlement. She could only have felt intense pressure and anxiety.

Then Lillian died in 2009 from leakage from the sinus cavity into her brain. My wonderful daughters sat by her bedside until she expired at 80 years old. They all had their special relationship with Lillian. Her death caused immense sadness. Lillian was a vastly loving and caring mother.

As mentioned above, Leigh's oldest son Austin, 22 years old, died of a drug overdose, Aug 5, 2012. The shock, pain, and sorrow were almost overwhelming for Leigh. I write about Austin in Chapter 9, Grandchildren.

Leigh returned to work and went to some grief groups. Her wonderful sweetie Rich was there to comfort her. We in the family fear asking her how she is doing because that will bring up the sadness. Yet if we don't ask, she may think we are not caring. She has a fine job as an administrator at the Yale Medical School. She is active at her Trinity Church and works with a program feeding the hungry.

Sarah has had a good decade. She too suffered after Lillian's death. She has continued her work as a pediatric critical care nurse at Massachusetts General Hospital in Boston. She has worked there almost since she graduated from nursing school. Her daily commute by car from Andover was marred by an auto accident.

I got an email from Sarah saying that she wanted us to hear it from her that she had been in an auto accident. The event was already on the radio news. Driving to work in the early morning dark, her car hit a car stopped and only partially pulled off the highway. Her car spun around and she was OK but shocked. A woman got out of her car to see if Sarah was all right and she was hit by another oncoming car and subsequently died. Sarah's car was totally wrecked. I saw pictures of her ruined car and could only thank God that Sarah was safe and so saddened that the other woman, also a nurse, had died.

Jessica has wonderful women friends. They visit each other regularly, travel and correspond with each other.

Children and Ann

My daughters and Ann have had a good relationship since we married in 1983. Since I retired, their relationship has grown closer. Sarah said that she was so very happy that Ann and I have such a loving relationship over the years. She said she saw how much we loved each other and meant to each other. She also said she was glad Ann had made me so happy.

After Lillian's death in 2009, the divided loyalty they had toward Lillian and me changed and they have been more open and affectionate toward Ann. The Thanksgiving dinners are one huge example. Last summer Leigh and Rich joined Ann and me in our Utah cabin for a few days. Jessica and Ben, Sarah and Rich joined us at the Bishop's ranch in Healdsburg, CA for a few days. It was wonderful that all three couples joined us in the west for part of their vacations.

Ann has always been fond of my girls. She remembers their birthdays and those of their children. She always wants any news I have of them.

I am very happy to have the love and affection of my daughters and certainly that of Ann.

CHAPTER 9

GRANDCHILDREN

While the grandchildren were babies and growing up, I called myself grandfather-lite. I would wipe nothing below the chin. Worst of all I hated to read to them those ditsy storybooks that bored me to the jeepers. I did like to do the crossword puzzles with them at breakfast.

Now that I am in my golden years and retired, I discover they have grown up.

Sarah's Mary Charlotte and Eric

Sarah's son Eric has graduated from high school and Johns Hopkins University and is on his way to employment in a Boston consulting firm.

In March of 2016 I was very surprised to get an email from Eric. He wanted to come to San Francisco and stay with me. He knew Ann was travelling in Patagonia at that time. I was pleased and flattered that he wanted to come. He slept on the floor in a sleeping bag, drove my yellow 14-year-old Volkswagen New Beetle to sightsee and visit friends. He came to hear me preach at St. John's, joined me for breakfast and a couple of dinners. He brought a high school friend, Tracy, to dinner one evening. She is finishing at Cal Berkeley. She is a vegetarian and created a marvelous salad.

Eric was mostly silent. He answered my questions and seldom

asked me anything about my life and work. He was mostly texting on his iPhone. I wanted more conversation but that was not his way on this visit. He graduated from Johns Hopkins in 2006.

Sarah's daughter Mary Charlotte has graduated from high school and Stonehill College in Easton, MA. She has been employed in the administration of Mass General.

Mary Charlotte always has been cheerful and lively. Intense interest in the Barbara C. Harris Camp of the Diocese of Massachusetts formed her interest in the church. She went as a camper and then became a counselor. When she graduated from college, she was too old to be a camp staff person. She continues active in Diocesan Youth work. She even got a part time job as youth director of a suburban Boston Episcopal Church.

After graduating from Stone Hill College, MC and some of her friends pooled their money and rented a house together near Boston. She is independent without being self-righteous. She and Sarah get along as friends and enjoy each other's company pretty much as equals.

In March of 2016, Sarah, MC and Jessica met me in Phoenix, Arizona at the Wigwam Resort. (Pardon the political incorrectness.) The women got along as equals. I never saw anything that made me think they were mother, aunt, and child, but only friends. I think it is a remarkable and wonderful relationship that they have together.

MC is blond, with blue eyes, fair skin, and a bit plump. She seems absolutely at home in her body. She walked around the Phoenix pool in her bikini with no self-consciousness or embarrassment about her body. I was very proud of her. She is smart, quick with words, and a delight to be with.

Jessica's Caleb

Jessica's son Caleb has graduated from Bates College in Maine, and is employed in Hartford, CT. Ben and Jessica had a bump in their marriage after Caleb left home for Bates. They faced the empty nest where before they had been full time parents. Ben spent a few months in Wyoming with his sisters and good friend. Time seemed to have healed the relationship and they are back together happily now.

Caleb and I have had little conversation or contact. He is always pleasant and polite. Perhaps that is just the way with an 85-year-old grandpa and a young man in his 20s.

Leigh's Daniel, Catherine, and Austin

Catherine was at Boston University then transferred to the University of Connecticut. I was so proud of her when she won an opportunity to do a year abroad in Bosnia. She loved it.

Daniel is on a break from college, living home with Leigh, and has a job in New Haven. He is uncertain about his future. A couple of summers ago he worked at the Camp where Mary Charlotte was employed. I thought it was great and congratulated him for having fun. Most of the family was not pleased.

Austin

The late Austin Lindsay, Leigh's son, who died August 4, 2014, was my first grandchild. He died at the age of 22 of a drug overdose.

He was chubby, funny and smart. After I retired in 2002, he was in high school and beginning to get involved in drugs. He was a user and a seller. He lost a lot of weight very fast; he probably was on speed. He had a cute blond girlfriend. He got busted at least once. He went to the University of Connecticut where he apparently made money selling drugs. Experimenting with heroin, he accidently ended his life. He was a good kid, jolly, and had a great future, sadly cut short by drugs.

Here is something I wrote five years after Austin's death:

It was cool in the morning and I was just getting up in our cabin at Brighton, Utah.

Leigh called. She said, Daddy, Austin has died.

Jesus, Mary, and Joseph, I exhaled into the phone. What happened?

He was found dead in his room near UCONN. Drugs maybe. I don't know much else.

I am so sorry I wailed, over and over again.

Ann came into the bedroom asking what happened. I told her. She began to cry.

I then said to Leigh, "We will come to New Haven as soon as we can get a plane."

I sat with Ann in the big living room with the morning sun creeping in. We talked about Austin, my first grandson and my daughter Leigh's first born. I could not get the thought of Leigh's immense sadness out of my mind.

We got to New Haven a few days later. The funeral was set for Monday, August 15, 2011.

Leigh asked me to preach the funeral sermon. I was pleased and horrified. The church was packed. Austin had been a choir boy for many years. Leigh was very active in the parish and had served on the vestry.

Sermon at the Requiem Eucharist
in memory of Austin Alexander Lindsay
in Trinity Church, New Haven, CT.
on Monday, August 15, 2011
Given by The Rev. Robert Warren Cromey
Priest retired of the Episcopal Church

Austin Lindsay was my first grandson. His mother, Leigh Cromey is my first daughter.

Funerals are not to celebrate life. Funerals are times and places to mourn, to feel sad, to feel guilty, and express our sorrow. Funerals are a time to allow yourself to be a mess.

The best way to move from pain and sorrow is to allow that guilt, allow, that sadness, cry those tears. Keep allowing that suffering to just be there. Of course, you go to work, take care of the kids, and have a martini. Grieving is a gift from God, a precious gift that moves us toward healing and new life.

I baptized Austin in 2001 at Trinity Church, San Francisco, California when I was rector there.

Austin was the perfect bouncing baby boy. The ready smile, the relentless competitor. Once when he was five I went for a walk with him. He kept attacking me, as boys tend to do as a way of expressing affection. He charged up to me, grabbed me, I unpeeled his arm and pushed him away and he fell down. He got right up and attacked me again. I pushed him down and he got up, ran at me again. This happened at least a dozen times. His chubby little legs kept charging at grandpa Robert. Now I know why I had to have knee replacements.

When we had breakfast together, I would do the crossword puzzle and Austin and his brother Daniel and sister Catherine vied for the right word. Austin would hate it if his sister thought of a word first. But he loved to do them with me.

Austin and his family joined Ann and me in Puerto Vallarta, Mexico one winter. Ann took them on a hike past some the very poor and hungry people by a stream. Austin told me he was glad he had an opportunity to see such poverty at first hand. He was exhilarated to join his dad on a parachute ride that carried him high over the city and the bay.

Austin was a choirboy here in this church until his voice changed. He was quite fetching in his red robe and stiff collar.

He liked good novels and he, my wife Ann, and Almariet his girl girlfriend discussed books together the last time Ann and I saw Austin.

Then there was college and drugs. Then Austin died.

Many scientists tell us that when we die, we are dead, it's over. That is all there is. But science is not the only way of knowing. From time immemorial, poets have sung of life after death. Homer, Dante, Milton. Wordsworth wrote of Intimations of Immortality. Great music moves us to celebrate that death is not end of life. Listen to Bach's B Minor Mass for instance. Many of us have an instinct about life eternal.

We Christians here in this church have a sure and certain hope in resurrection and new life. Our hope and belief is that Austin is in the hands of a loving God. Of course, we can't prove that empirically. But that is our faith. That hope is based on our Christian story of the death and resurrection of Jesus. Jesus died because he was a revolutionary. The religious and political leaders feared him because of his radical ideas. He preached that we need to feed the hungry, heal the sick, free the oppressed, and stand for peace. So Jesus died on the cross. We believe he rose again from the dead at Easter. We believe his resurrection means that all of us survive our mortal deaths, life continues in mystical and new ways that we do not understand.

Austin died because of illegal drugs. They affect the lives of millions of people in this country and around the world.

I hope we go out of this church with a renewed determination to find creative ways to control illegal drugs. All the ways are complex and controversial but drugs are affecting our young people.

I hope we go out of this church in memory of Austin to find ways to end drug trafficking.

I hope we go out of this church in memory of Austin to help all young people resist illegal drugs.

Austin, we are with you 'til we meet again.

Austin, "God be with you 'til we meet again."

From the New Haven Register

LINDSAY, AUSTIN ALEXANDER Austin Alexander Lindsay, aged 20, died unexpectedly on Thursday night, August 4, in his apartment in Mansfield Connecticut. His friends and family will remember him for his humor and wit, generosity and selfless hospitality towards people he met. He was an avid reader, a graduate from Hamden High School in 2008, and he was enrolled at the University of Connecticut in Storrs. He is survived by his parents, David Lindsay and Leigh Cromey, and his siblings Daniel and Catherine in Hamden, CT. There will be a Memorial Service on Monday, August 15 at 5 PM at Trinity Episcopal Church on the Green in New Haven, on the corner of Temple and Chapel.

A letter about Austin

Austin Lindsay died a year ago today, August 4, 2015.

Dear Family and Friends,

This is a sad day for all of us, Leigh and David particularly. Ann and I send you our most heartfelt sympathies, thoughts and prayers. I write from Brighton, Utah knowing that Leigh will be surrounded by her sisters, Sarah and Jessica, and a host of family relatives and friends this weekend.

I shall never forget the outpouring of love and sympathy to Leigh after Austin's death was told to us all. You gathered from all over to send you concern and feelings and attend the funeral at Trinity Church, New Haven.

I wrote this to Leigh. "Last year I gathered lots of old prints, tossed many and put the rest into two albums. I took all the ones of Austin I could find and put them into one photo album along with others. I look at them from time to time and realize how much I miss him. I always had the fantasy that he would produce my first great-grand child."

Leigh has told me how many of you have kept in touch with her over the past year. Your support and love, I am sure have sustained her and her family.

Ann and I will provide flowers at the altar of our parish in San Francisco on August 12, 2012, to the greater glory of God and in memory of Austin Lindsay.

With love and gratitude to you all,

Robert and Ann too

Sadness passes slowly. But life continues.

My grandchildren are now pleasant distant friends. I am delighted to see them from time to time. They are well launched into their own lives and careers.

Daniel is taking a vacation from Green Mountain College after three and a half years. Mary Charlotte finished Stone Hill. Caleb graduated Bates and Eric is finished at John's Hopkins.

All of the grandchildren have visited San Francisco except for Caleb. He'll be out here on business soon, I expect. They are adults and I think of them that way. I do not give them advice unless they specifically ask for it. I have the same policy with my daughters and in fact with all the people I know.

Another way to think about advice is this; Give people lots of advice, they seldom follow it. Advise someone to jump off the Golden Gate Bridge. They won't follow your advice, so give it anyway. Knowing that, I seldom give advice unless someone asks me for it. Even then I warn them that they probably won't follow it. I suppose giving advice helps people gather lots of advice and then choose their own course based on the information they have gathered. The giver of advice often feels better, helpful and needed. That is fine, but realize advice's limitations.

I used to enjoy sending my grandchildren checks for their birthdays, graduations and Christmas. I loved it that their mothers insisted they write thank you notes. No thank you notes, no checks. That is my motto.

I don't care what the current non-manners are. We send wedding gifts and seldom get thank you notes. That's the last time they get a gift from me. Ann, however, is a much nicer and more thoughtful person than me. She will send a present any time she wants. Great for her. When people apply for jobs, they better send thank you notes to a person who interviews them. Not only is it good manners but also good business. Even if you don't get hired, the employer may remember your note and name and pass it on to someone else who might hire you.

I like to point out that any nine months from now I could become a great-grandfather.

A Quiet Moment

Ann and I

Babes in Pulpit

Church of St. John the Evangelist SF

Edwin, Dad and I

Philene, Mary Charlotte and I

Sarah, Jessica, Brother Edwin, Leigh, Pamela

Leigh Cromey

Ann and Robert

Three Daughters on my 80th Birthday

Two Fathers at Baptism

Vigil for Peace and Justice

RETIREMENT TRAVEL

Ann likes to travel a lot. I like to travel a bit. Travel for Ann is learning, expansion of consciousness, adventure, seeing as many places as possible and enjoying them all. I like to travel to places that are historical for me—England and Europe. The Church I know and care about got refined and ruined in Europe. Ann had travelled in Europe long before we married but she was willing to go again to London, Paris, Rome, Venice, Barcelona, and Madrid.

Right after I retired from Trinity in 2002, we spent two weeks in Puerto Vallarta, Mexico. We did our usual reading, eating, and walking about. Ann did some hiking. In the evenings, we enjoyed walking along the Malecon, watching the mix of tourists, natives of Mexico, and townspeople. It was a welcome break and transition from the festivities surrounding my retirement.

Blackmail

In 2007, I wanted to travel in Europe in the fall when there is the best weather. Ann said I should wait until next summer. I wanted to go in the fall. She wanted to teach another year. I said, "OK you teach for another year and I'll go to Europe by myself and visit some of my old girl friends who live in Europe now.

I met Nadine in 1963, the year after I came to San Francisco. She became interested in the Civil Rights Movement. An interior designer, she also had a husband and three boys. She is lively, funny and creative. After her divorce, she became a therapist and group leader in the United States and Europe, and now lives in Portugal. She is a woman of few husbands and many lovers.

Janice came to groups I led in Chicago in the 1970s. Small, dark and sexy, I often stayed in her apartment when I was in Chicago. We stayed in contact over the yeas. When she heard Ann and I were going to marry she wrote, "Congratulations but I thought you and I were going to get married." Janice lives in Scotland now with her husband Arnold..

Ingrid was my banker and lover for the year I lived in Germany 1977-78.. Small, very smart and generous, she translated my English into German when I lead groups for the parents of drug addict patients I worked with. Ingrid lives in Neus, Germany with her husband, Wolfgang and daughter.

She thought for a while and said, "OK I'll retire and we can go to Europe in the fall together."

Sure enough we did go to visit my old women friends and had a delightful time with them and their spouses or lovers.

Ingrid and Wolfgang lived near Cologne. We stayed five days in their lovely suburban home. We visited the great Cologne Cathedral. Then we went to Holland to visit Janice and Arnold, his homeland. We also visited Nadine Scott in her summer home in Italy.

Queen Mary 2

In 2014, Ann and I made a round trip crossing on the Queen Mary 2 from Brooklyn, NY, to Southampton, England. We stayed in the Chelsea area of London in a small flat for a month and returned to the United States. Crossing the Atlantic on a fine ship was a long hankering of mine. It was touched with the idea that Grandpa

Cromey, my father's father crossed from England to the United States in the late 19th Century. My mother's family, the Reinemanns, left Germany for America in the early 19th century.

I also wanted to have the experience of sailing on a luxurious ocean liner. Stories and movies had romanticized such a voyage for me.

We flew from San Francisco to New York, stayed one night in a Brooklyn hotel and boarded the liner the next morning. Since I was born in Brooklyn, I thought it a just coincidence that we left for England from that borough, rather than the more elegant sounding "sailing from New York."

The enormous black hull, high as an apartment house, was painted red at the waterline. High above was the bright white of the rest of the ship with its windowed cabins, wooden decks, and mysterious control towers.

We hated the usual hassles of getting on, filling out health forms, giving and receiving passports, credit cards, getting keys, receipts, going

this way and that-a-way, waiting in line, shuffling ahead, finally landing in our cabin. Nick our cabin boy went on and on about the shower, TV which we never watched, the bed, the deck, the blah and the blah. All I wanted to do was to lie down and take off my shoes, which I did and fully dressed lay in the bed while he continued and concluded reciting the most obvious endlessly.

Our cabin was compact and comfortable with an outside view. I enjoyed the tiny toilet, shower basin and mirror that could close off for privacy. The closets were ample and the queen-sized bed most comfortable. The tan colors of the ceiling and walls gave off plenty of light. There were also a small couch and easy chair and coffee table between the bed and the glass door leading out to the balcony with its outdoor ocean view.

We began to explore the ship, finding the cafeteria for a fine lunch with endless choices of meats, salads, hot and cold food, beverages, and desserts. We found a table next to the windows so as to enjoy the views, which were mostly vast water and dark clouds. More investigation led us to the theater, library, gym, main dining room, cocktail lounges, and gambling parlor.

When we set sail in the late afternoon, we watched Manhattan, the Statue of Liberty, and the harbor islands become part of the wake of the huge ship.

We went to dinner in the elegantly decorated main dining room. In the elevator, I groused when Ann flicked my lapel. I said, I hate having dandruff brushed off. The bald man standing next to me said, "Well, at least you have dandruff." The dining room had lots of gold hangings, gold framed mirrors, and golden railings supporting us up and down to decorated tables. They had fresh flowers, fine china, silverware, and glasses. Waiters were cool, efficient, and helpful.

We had chosen seating so that we were with three other couples each evening. The people were mostly pleasant but there was one weird woman I hid from whenever I saw her. She knew everyone, had been everywhere, had taken fifty cruises, and told us at great length about them if she could catch us.

Thrice we dressed formally for dinner. Ann in a long and lovely dress and I in my tux. Breakfast and lunch we ate in the cafeteria where we had a wide selection of food. The problem always was trying not to eat too much.

Lots of wonderful meals tempted us, a great variety of breakfast opportunities: fresh milk, cereals, eggs, bacon, ham, sausage, rolls, croissant, cold cuts, Kippers, grilled tomatoes, fresh fruit, cheeses and on and on. Lunch and breakfast is cafeteria style, dinner at a table of eight.

Lunch: soups, salads, lousy sushi, roast ham, roast beef, and all the fixings. Shrimp and smoked salmon salads, salad bar with everything on it you can imagine.

Three-course dinners with soups, terrines of this and that, salads, main course choices of fowl, meat, and fish. Vegetables. I had haddock one night and duck breast the next. Portions were small and satisfying. The variety of desserts including cakes, creams and cheeses charmed us.

The second day out high winds, and gales someone said. The ship was a bit rocky. Walking reminded me a bit of how I feel after a martini or three. I felt like a weaving drunk and I had not even brushed my teeth. Hardy souls walked deck at 7am. Three round trips on that deck gives us a mile. We did it one day, but it was too windy for this frail mariner that or any day.

Royal Shakespeare Co. was on board for performances and theater games workshops, which we enjoyed greatly. The actors got us passengers up, moving, presenting skits, plays, and exercises.

Concerts, lectures, movies, and nightclub shows entertained us every moment of the day if we wished to attend. I read a lot. People were pleasant and friendly. They were from all over the world and some had been on the ship from Southampton to New York and returned immediately just enjoying the 14 days on board.

The QM2 library was quite small and cramped although the shiny, lacquered book cases with bright yellow brass fittings were quite elegant. The room had good views, but the mystery and novel sections were full of airport style best sellers.

The weather was mostly cloudy with only two days warm enough to sit out on the deck. We certainly got a look at the vastness of the sea and sky. A month later the return trip was also a delight.

We were awed by the inevitability of the vast sea as we cruised along. The sea changes colors of blue and gray with snatches of white foam.

We went to a ship board movie called *Rushmore*. On going down the stairs to our seats, I fell gracefully, I'm told. I did not pass out, just was stunned. My shoulder and hands broke the fall. I had small bruises on my right cheek and knee. Otherwise I was fine. Men rushed to my side, made me sit for a while, helped me stand. I was not dizzy or hurt and took my seat. I felt fine by the time the movie started and forgot about it until people checked with me afterward to see if I was OK. I was. I thought the movie rather stupid.

Here are some bits from my ship board diary

Tuesday, June 17, 2014

We awakened to calm seas and bright sunshine. The ship was steadier than yesterday during gale force winds. After breakfast, we walked around the deck twice together and Ann went on for another round making it a one mile walk for her. I felt good that I walked so far without pain and not much fatigue. We realized we had just three more days on the ship before we get to Southampton.

Thursday, June 19, 2014

This is our last day at sea. We did some mime games at the RADA show this morning. I enjoyed this thrice-given workshop most on board ship. We did theater warm-ups; character exercises and mood tries. It was interactive fun and thoughtful. I feel the Spa talks were too frequent and always selling rings at the highest prices. Mani-pedis $99.00. In SF I pay 23.00 plus a $5.00 tip. I'd like more interactive activities on the ship.

Weather was lovely and clear most of the day, but quite windy. I made it twice around the ship walking. Ann again did three times, thus a mile.

I sat on deck for a while but it was really too windy to enjoy. Looking at the Atlantic Ocean I realize its vastness. So much of the earth is made up of the oceans. The waves are interesting for a while. The rolling, the white caps, churning and the depths and then the heights of the waves delight. Two miles deep we were told the other day. The captain said that there were whole mountain ranges under the waters. The colors were deep blues, sometimes black and then aqua close to the ship.

I noticed today how many men walk with some limp or halting gait. Myself included. I am still shocked at how obese some people get, women mostly, but plenty of fat men too. Of course, we are mostly elderly people.

Last night we went to a dance and music show for an hour or so. We did see some fantastic dancing and acrobatics. The men and women performers are in fantastic physical shape, slender and well-made bodies, and some good singing too. Music of the forties and fifties pleased the crowd. Normally, I don't like these shows, but did enjoy these.

We enjoyed our month in Chelsea. We visited London museums, gardens, and galleries. We saw lots of Hugh and Stephen. We met them the summer I was in residence at St. James's, Piccadilly. We stayed with them on other visits to England. We had a fine dinner with Bonnie and Steve. When Bonnie lived in San Francisco, she sang in the Trinity choir.

We took an awful bus ride to Oxford. It stopped at every bus stop in London and several stops en route. We went to see the sights in Oxford and visit Mansfield College where we stayed and where Ann had studied T.S. Eliot and Thomas Hardy when she won a National Endowment for the Arts scholarship in 1988. We also had a delightful lunch with Nick and Sally. Nick had recently retired as an English master at Eton College.

Home Alone

Ann took some long trips without me. She is always anxious when she had to leave me alone for great lengths of time. I no longer want to take long airplane rides. I often get sick when travelling, so I prefer to stay home in our lovely flat in San Francisco. She is afraid I might die while she is away. I fear she might die travelling in exotic places. She is fearless.

In France one time, I had an ischemic attack and spent an

overnight in the hospital. In 2015 in Madrid, I was sick at my stomach for two whole days. In 2025, in Chicago I had a horrible flu attack and went to the Emergency Room at Northwestern Hospital for a few hours. These little skirmishes with my health make me more than leery of travelling far from home.

Ann went to Cuba, Vietnam, Bhutan, Brazil, and Patagonia with a friend or a tour group. Three weeks away is what we have agreed upon as acceptable.

I enjoy a lot of time alone. While Ann is away I try to have lunch or dinner with someone every other day. The other days I am happy to have a cocktail and a small home cooked dinner by myself. I read and watch movies on Netflix in the evenings.

I generally get up early, read the paper, do some exercises, not too much, write my 500 words, go for a walk, shop, nap and get ready for the evenings.

I always miss Ann, but not achingly. I think of her often and she is always in my prayers of thanksgiving, as are my daughters and family. Sometimes I am happy that I don't have to interact with Ann or anyone. I don't have to answer a lot of questions, be concerned about her whereabouts, and don't bump into her in the narrow hallway of our flat. I listen to music without fear of waking her up from her nap.

I take a short trip to Palm Springs to visit friends there. I have met my daughters in St. Petersburg, Florida and Phoenix, Arizona, for a gettogether where it is warm or even hot.

One amusing part of hearing that I will be alone while Ann is away: people say, "I'll bring a casserole." "We'll have you over for dinner." "We'll call you to see that you are all right." None of them ever do. It really is quite fine with me because I do enjoy this alone time.

More Trips

Our trips to New England were to visit my daughters and their families. Leigh lives in New Haven, CT, Jessica in Litchfield, CT, and Sarah in Boston. It is always a pleasure to visit with them for meals, walks, restaurants, and talks. Beginning in 2013 we have had Thanksgiving Dinner at one of the girls' homes, rotating through their dinner tables. My daughters were there with whatever grandchildren could be rustled up and husband or sweetie of the girls. Dinners were always lush with brown turkey and all the trimmings and pies and wine.

We often then spent a few days in New York City at the Roosevelt Hotel, and dining with old friends who live in New York. Brother Edwin and Pamela entertained us or we them during our time in the East. People ask us what shows did we see? We don't go to the theater, we dine with several friends who had moved to New York after we met in San Francisco. Robin and Beth, Gio Tusa, Ed and David and their children Emma and Luke, Rob, and Karla.

We also take an annual trip for two weeks to Brighton, Utah, high above Salt Lake City. We stay in a cabin we own with Ann's family and spend two weeks in August there. At the cabin, we entertain the families of Ann's brothers. It is usually a big gathering as there are many offspring. Ann hikes and I walk around Silver Lake as well as shop and cook. We also have other friends from Salt Lake whom we often entertain. Larry and Wendy Foster-Leigh, Jim and George.

Going shopping for food near the cabin is always an adventure. First it is downhill for a half hour to get to the shopping center. Since I drive slowly, I have to pull over a lot to let the fast drivers zoom on by.

Then there is the choice of which store to spend my money in for groceries. Dan's is local but probably owned by Mormons and I don't want to support them. Then there is Whole Foods, which is non-union and high priced. I am not a true believer that organic is any better for you that the regular stuff.

The cabin is set in the midst of tall Aspens. A little walk gives us views of the surrounding mountains. Lots of flora and fauna all over the place.

Here is a gross list of the places we have traveled

2003 – Mexico, Utah, Tahoe, New York City

2004 – Puerto Vallarta, Paris, NYC

2005 – Ann to Cuba; We to Brighton, Canada, NYC

2006 – PV, Atlanta, Ann to Copper Canyon

2007 – London, Amsterdam, Germany, Venice, Treviso, Rome, NYC

2008 – New Haven, Andover, Boston

2009 – San Miguel, Atlanta, Savannah, Charleston, Washington, NYC, Tuxedo Park, Litchfield, New Haven, Andover Boston. Ann went to Vietnam and Cambodia. We went to Paris, Barcelona, Madrid, and PV.

2011 – Ashland, New Haven—Austin's funeral.

2012 – Ann to Bhutan

2013 – Holland American to PV, Sacramento, Ann to Brazil

2015 – Chicago, Clear Lake, Pt. Reyes, Bishop's Ranch.

2016 – Ann went to Patagonia. I went to Palm Springs and Phoenix.

2017 – We have booked for a Viking River Cruise, June 29-July 14, then the Utah Cabin, August 1-14

CHAPTER 10

MEMORIES OF TRINITY

Thanks for the Memories was the theme song of the late comedian Bob Hope. I am very happy with my memories, even the not so good ones. Writing about the decade-plus since I "graduated" from my work as rector of Trinity Episcopal Church, San Francisco lifted to my mind mostly lovely thoughts and recollections. Memories can inspire or bore people including oneself. There are some sad ones as well as ecstatic ones, quiet gentle ones, or quietly hilarious ones.

I love my nostalgia streak, thinking of the good old times in my life. Even the painful memories often teach me things. I suppose memories can interfere with love and work. If an inordinate amount of time is spent ruminating about the past, that activity can get in the way of interactive relationships with others. It can prevent enjoying projects, hobbies, sports and just doing the chores necessary for pleasant living. I suspect compulsive living in the past can be depressing or perhaps a sign of depression.

However, a person with no sense of the past, not enjoying the past or fleeing the pain of the past, cannot have a fully mature personality.

I remember the roar of applause and cheers as I proceeded out of the church at the conclusion of my final service there. I did not want to stop my tears.

The day started with a great fuck with Ann, always fun, invigorating and as the saying goes, start each day with a good lay. It was celebration number one on the final day of my rectorship of Trinity. The big service and party lay ahead.

Breakfast and off to the church for the last time as Rector. Driving up Franklin Street I think gladly and sadly about this my last trip to the church, the last time I pull into my parking space—reserved.

In the rector's class I talk about the Phillip and Carl episode where Carl uses a chain saw to cut off Philip's foot.

Then I tell the story of the unholy Trinity, a couple of Jean Cathcart stories and how we lost Project Open Hand as a Trinity program. Thirty people come to hear the stories.

I went upstairs to my office to vest for the service. Armand, Michael, Forrest, Rob, Elizabeth were there. The volunteer clergy dated back 15 of the 20 years I have been at Trinity.

I wanted them there to honor them and thank them and to show the congregation the continuity of clergy support for our ministry. I am proud that I had the willingness to take on openly gay and lesbian clergy long before they were welcomed into more main line churches.

There was a grand procession around the church—crosses, banners, flags, huge choir, all the acolytes, clergy, and I at the end. It was a show of strength of the parish and of the church. Processions are symbols of movement, development, and going ahead into a new phase of my life and Trinity's.

We sang my favorite hymns. The Lyric Chorus augmented the Trinity choir so there were 30 choristers. They sang selections from Mozart and Bach. Sandy and Deborah sang a selection from Cantata 76 by Bach. This is one of my favorite duets for soprano and alto. They blew me a kiss when it was over. It was a day of gorgeous music and singing.

Lois Webb read the piece about time from Ecclesiastes. Rob Droste read the Gospel from the Sermon on the Mount.

I preached the following sermon on time:

★   ★   ★

Time
Trinity Episcopal Church
Final Sermon as Rector of Trinity
2/17/02

This is the swan song of a lame duck.

This is my final sermon. It is about time. Or as some would say, "It's about time."

Just to keep things in perspective, let me remind you that Michael Jordan is 39 today.

One of the nicest things Robert Kitzman ever said to me was that I was a fine Biblical scholar. "No matter what the Biblical text, Cromey can always turn it around to be a sermon on gay rights."

20 years and four months is a long time and a short time.

Where has the time gone? Time flies. Time after time. "Time like an ever-rolling stream."

Good times. Time and again. Time and tide wait for no one. Timely. Good times, past times, time-to-time, time of my life,

Time stood still—I stood in front of a TV set in NYC on Sept. 11, 2001 and watched the planes go into those buildings and then later saw the buildings collapse. Time stood still. Times since have changed.

Timely, untimely. Time to retire and time to leave Trinity as its Rector.

God's time. God, the ground of all being. God, being itself, God is beyond time. God creates time and transcends it. God sees our beginning and end and our future and the future of the universe all at once. Our time is fourscore years and ten. We have our time and love our time, but God's time stretches far beyond our feeble attempt to comprehend time or to capture our time.

My friend Armand Kreft asked me what I was most proud of in my ministry. I replied, "The times I and others worked for full freedom for African Americans and homosexuals in our country and church." I felt moved by the Holy Spirit at those times.

I am grateful for the opportunity and the gift from God to work for justice in and through the church. That time was not wasted. That time spent is what the message of Jesus is all about.

These 20 years have been times of great joy. My marriage to Ann right here at Trinity on August 14, 1983. During these 20 years, all three of my daughters married and have given me six grandchildren.

My work as Rector has been a great joy. Preaching, teaching, marrying, burying, baptizing, celebrating Eucharist, visiting people in my office, in homes and hospitals. Laughing singing, praying, and seeing people get what the Gospel is all about. When one is happy in work and love, one is truly joyous.

To be happy in love and work is the recipe for joyful living.

We Christians are called to follow Jesus. I have led this parish in proclaiming love, forgiveness, justice, care for the poor and hungry, to live by faith and not the law. We worship God in the beauty of holiness.

Last week was the birthday of Abraham Lincoln. I read over the Gettysburg Address given in 1863 and the Second inaugural address given in 1865. His most famous words have meaning for us now.

In a time when we have the results of a curious election of the present incumbent of the White House, see the insidious intervention of big business into electoral politics and the fact that 60% of the people of the United States fail to vote, we need to remember Lincoln's words. "That this nation, under God, shall have a new birth of freedom—and that the government of the people, by the people, and for the people shall not perish from the earth."

In a time when we are at war with an unspecific enemy, bombing poor and hungry people, threatening other nations, we yearn for an end. Lincoln's words ring out. "With malice toward none; with charity for all; with firmness for the right, as God gives us to see the right, let us strive on to finish the work we are in; to bind up the nation's wounds; to care for them who shall have borne battle, for the widow and orphan—to do all which may achieve and cherish a just and lasting peace among ourselves and with all nations."

This is a time for my gratitude.

For the love and support of the congregation over these 20 years.

For the freedom you have given me to be outspoken on the great issues of our time in my preaching and writing. HIV Aids, homosexual rights, anti-capital punishment, feeding and sheltering the homeless, the Israel-Palestinian awfulness and antiwar statements.

For Ann for putting up with me all these years. For my daughters who love me.

For this beautiful building and our music, the space and sound, since our worship is so important to our health and happiness.

It is time for the future:

Rob Droste our Interim Rector takes the leadership in these months ahead during the search for a new Rector. Support him, serve him, love him, and let him love you, serve you and support you.

The Wardens and Vestry and members of the parish to lead and take responsibility for the growth and stability of the building and congregation.

It is time to continue to bring the message of God in Christ into the world—hungry in stomach and hungry soul for the good news of love, forgiveness, compassion, and justice.

Thank you for our time together.

★　★　★

At the end of my sermon the congregation gave me a prolonged standing ovation. I wiped and wiped my tears and applause kept right on coming. I revel in applause. It is so wonderful to have people show honor and respect in such a concerted and physical way. I remember some opera star saying, when asked what do you do all this singing for? She said, "The applause." It is true. Not many people are honored with sustained applause.

It is humbling because I know inside there is so much more I could have done. I did so little. Yet I did stand for some things before the issues became popular—civil rights for African Americans and homosexuals. I deserved the applause and I didn't. I am very happy that many people stood and gave their appreciation in that particular noisy way.

I decided that I wanted to give the bread of the communion to all who partake. I gave each person the bread and they peeled off and took the wine from the sub-deacons. It took a while but it was very moving to see so many people, old friends, many tears including my own. After the final hymn, the congregation again burst into long applause. Was a man ever so grateful and humbled by this honoring?

I stood at the narthex door and greeted, hugged, and shook hands with the 500 people as they left the church. Tears and clenched throats by me and many of them made it a truly joyous and profound moment.

John Sikorsky and Susan Mitchell, Bob and Maureen Sena, Rol Risska, the Wellbeloveds, Sandy and Andy, Ann Overton and on and on attended.

The luncheon and speeches afterward fed our bodies and souls. The late Michael Woodsmith said I was a kind man. The late John Michael Olexy said I failed him and he was mad at me because I didn't find him a boyfriend. Jose Sarria, the Widow Norton, said he felt just fine coming to Trinity dressed in her black weeds. Karen Raay said I made her talk about her personality while I was counseling her.

Bryan Farley said when he got home from work tired and hungry and his wife wanted something from him, he asked himself, "What would Cromey do?" Rob Droste said he appreciated my being a mentor to him and was grateful that he learned so much about parish life from my experience. Bob Sena said he appreciated that I emphasized that people must take responsibility for their own lives and also that I was tough on him and helped him get over his self-pity and get on with his life and that he met his present wife 25 years ago in my groups and I performed their wedding. Ann said I was a wonderful husband and very kind to her. She thanked the congregation for their love a support and told them she loved them and would miss them.

Sandy sang a lovely song about something and then sang the first verse of every hymn I chose that she hated. It was wildly funny for those of us on the inside of developing liturgy in the church. Rick Fabian said he was worried about what would happen to the Episcopal Church now that I had retired. He said he would have to keep a lifetime subscription to the Chronicle and Living Church "to read Robert's letters."

I was in a daze and very high when I left the church for the last time as rector. I kept losing things, getting into the wrong car. I lost my tear-wetted handkerchief. I had cards and presents and stuff from my office in my arms. Ann was there loving and supporting me. We drove home.

CHAPTER 12

SOCIAL AND POLITICAL ISSUES

Retirement years are always full of social and political issues. I have twice had the honor and privilege of voting for Barack Obama for President of the United States. Racial prejudice spoken and unspoken is still in the air. Our first African American president ran in primaries and the general election and race was a hidden issue. His mother was white. He chose to identify himself as an African American. Obama is a well-educated lawyer and community organizer, senator and then president. The bitter opposition to him from the Republican majority was in part because he was not white. I won't try to justify this statement as it has been voiced by many a pundit. I am not willing to do extensive research into the matter. It is my strong gut feeling, backed by other people's insights.

I hated that Obama rejoiced in murdering without trial Osama bin Laden. I strongly disagree with his condoning drone bombings, which killed so many civilians. His policy of continuing to deport illegal immigrants is deplorable. His continuing to send American troops into the Middle East just continues war and violence.

I have come to believe the U.S. should get out and stay out of the Middle East. Those countries had best work out their own problems. U.S. business interests, especially oil, keep getting American military killed, and millions of soldiers and civilians in Iraq, Afghanistan, Pakistan, and elsewhere murdered.

I rejoiced that he pushed through the Affordable Care Act allowing millions to get health insurance. He has reduced the deficit, strengthened the economy and reduced unemployment. I loved that he was a good father to his daughters and was a splendid orator.

The other hot issues of the last fifteen years have been killings by police officers, immigration rights, gun control, LGBT rights, the proliferation of transgender rights, and health.

Richard Leslie Smith, our Vicar at St. John's where Ann and I attend, is a hero in keeping alive the issue of cops killing young black and Latino men in the Mission District of San Francisco. Police officers are never convicted of killing their victims when and if the officers get to trial. Fr. Richard has helped us see clearly that the system is not bringing justice to the victims.

Richard also has kept us aware of the families broken apart by immigration policies sending a father or mother back to their home country because they are illegally resident in the United States. The government's policies wreck families, homes, and neighborhoods by this wanton deportation activity.

President Obama and many leaders have tried valiantly to pass legislation to prevent guns getting into the hands of people who are mentally or emotionally disturbed. Opposition by the right and the National Rifle Association has prevented such legislation. I write this just after a lone deranged gunman killed fifty people in an Orlando, Florida nightclub.

The transgender issue has arisen very strongly in the past decade. There have been men and women of some notoriety who have changed gender. Recently more people are making the change and saying so to their families and the public. The desire to change the sex one is born with is becoming more common. It has raised the issues of who is going to pay for the necessary surgery. How can traditional families adapt to the change in one of their members? Silly things as which toilets should be used. If a girl in an all-girl high school makes the change should he be able to remain in the school?

In addition, campuses continue to put women students at risk. Here is a sermon I preached on June 12, 2016 on the campus issue.

The Woman – Luke 7: 36-50

The woman shows Jesus great love by kissing his feet, bathing the road-weary feet, anointing them with oil and drying them with her hair. The woman is a sinner. Unmarried women in Jesus's day were in the depths of poverty. There were no welfare programs, food stamps, or soup kitchens. There is a good chance she was known as a prostitute.

Jesus was criticized by his host for allowing this woman to touch him, knowing she was a sinner. Men in Jesus's day did not even allow women to touch them.

Quote Jesus: Simon, do you see this woman? I entered your house; you gave me no water for my feet, but she has bathed my feet with her tears and dried them with her hair. You gave me no kiss, but from the time I came in she has not stopped kissing my feet. You did not anoint my head with oil, but she has anointed my feet with ointment. Therefore, I tell you her sins, which are many, have been forgiven: hence she has shown great love. But one, whom little is forgiven, loves little. Then he said to her, "Your sins are forgiven."

Men sat at the table, woman on the floor. But Jesus saw the woman as a human being. He raised her up and defended her to his host. He made her important. Jesus held women in high regard.

We Christians are called to treat women with high regard, dignity, and justice.

Treatment of women as second-class citizens, weak, and to be used results in RAPE.

Stanford raped woman, Jane Doe's story: She was drunk, assaulted and unconscious by by Brock Allen Turner after a fraternity party.

He got six months in jail for raping the unconscious co-ed. His father Dan Turner was quoted as saying "Why should his life be ruined for twenty minutes of action?" His statement followed Brock's light sentencing.

Sexism alive and miserable. 1 in 5 women will be sexually assaulted on college campuses. My granddaughter Catherine is a sophomore at Boston University. I worry about her.

Many straight men look upon women as sex objects, not persons.

Many gay men express hostility toward women.

Machismo is present among many Latino and black men.

Of course, many women regard all men as animals.

Prison systems turn a blind eye to men raping men in prisons, and women raping women.

Sex prejudice reigns in our culture.

Jesus associates with the woman. We followers of Jesus need to repent of our constant sexism and repent and beg forgiveness and then go out seeking love and justice for all.

Here is a Christian take away:

We all repent of our sexism toward women and men.

We can support legislation to treat raped women with respect.

We can support legislation that assures rapist will receive appropriate punishment and treatment.

We pray for Brock Allen Turner, the convicted rapist.

We pray for his father, Dan Turner, who callously said his son "should not be punished for 20 minutes of action."

We pray for Judge Aaron Pesky, who is vilified for his slap-on-the-wrist sentence of Brock Allen Turner.

We pray for the two Swedish bicyclists who helped Jane Doe survive the attack.

We pray for Jane Doe the victim of the rape, for her continued healing and restoration of her dignity.

We pray for ourselves that we avoid self-righteousness as we seek powerful justice for the victims of brutal crimes.

Friday, July 22, 2016

President Donald Trump was right in supporting conservative religious rights in his campaign. We liberals, secularists, and Democrats have consistently been snide, rude, and cruel to Christian believers. However, the thought of him being president is deplorable. He is certainly not to be trusted to control US nuclear weapons.

A hunky Jesus, a naked woman hanging on a cross, or artists urinating on the Madonna may not be blasphemous to you or me. We certainly do not want to ban these behaviors. Those activities profoundly hurt and pain many Christians and their beliefs.

A Hanukah candle and a manger scene in a public place are not a threat to the separation of church and state. Their symbolic expressions are not setting up a church or a national religion. They are an expression of religious tradition and a celebration of many religious Americans' heritage. Americans are a religious society. 70 percent of Americans say they believe in God. I have never heard of any of them wanting a state church or state religion.

Liberal Supreme Court Justices in the past held that public expressions of religion violated the separation of church and state. That is nonsense. Protestants and Catholics know they have been cruelly treated by the

Kings, Queens, and leaders of various countries in Europe, especially England, Spain and France. American believers have no interest in setting up a state church. That was the fear of the founding fathers as they made clear the separation of state and church. Separation of church and state does not mean the separation of religion and society.

Churches, synagogues, and mosques should have the right to freedom of public religious expression. Trump espouses that without an iota of knowing what he is talking about.

Prayers in school no.

Bible as literature in schools yes.

Choral music Choruses and Carols – yes.

Many of us Christians and liberal democrats were more than startled by the election of Donald Trump as president in 2016.

He is personally rude and obnoxious, unfit for the office and is a racist demagogue.

The outpouring of hate and incivility poured upon him by much of the mass and social media has been horrific. While I plan to resist his cruel and misanthropic policies, as a serious Christian, I regard him as a human being, deeply flawed. But why the hate, the anxiety and paranoia?

There is real danger afloat by our present leadership. But why the worry, the unease, the passionate distrust? Watching the president and his gang on TV is the culprit. Every moment spent watching the lords of misrule burn into our eyeballs and brains hateful long-lasting images damages us. The more we watch, the more these people influence our anxiety and us. Get our news from newspapers, not TV or computer screens. Reading the newspaper allows us to pick and choose what and how much news we want to see. On TV we are at the mercy of the newscasters, advertisers and politicians whose images etch into our brains. Newspapers and the printed word set us free to choose. Newspapers manipulate, too. But we can read or not. On TV we have to take what we get.

CHAPTER 13

MY RELIGIOUS CONSCIOUSNESS

Here is how I look at my theology in my retirement years. My religious beliefs have developed, grown, and changed over the years.

Spirituality and Secularism are two streams of the American consciousness in this decade of the 21st Century. Secularism is the notion that God, churches, and religion are of little or no value in one's daily life. Science, technology, and individualism are all one needs to get along in the world.

Spirituality holds that there is a God. Churches teach and live the story of the Bible, and the Christian tradition and religion respect and are interested in the wide variety of ways of worship and ethical principles.

There is a stream of spiritualty which proclaims not to be religious, but spiritual. This group may acknowledge a level of being beyond human experience.

In this somewhat simple view of the religious and secular world, I ask myself, how did I become a religious person?

My father was a priest of the Episcopal Church. A picture hangs in our hallway of my father in his vestments proudly standing with his arms around his two sons, Bobby and Edwin (my younger brother). We are standing in a doorway of Emmanuel Church on Long Island.

Dad is enfolding his sons in his vestments. This picture was taken in 1939.

We went to church on Sundays. Often, we went to Sunday School classes with other kids. We were acolytes or altar boys for our father. I always liked those activities. Being an altar boy was a way of showing off and being seen. I never felt any deep feeling or emotion about church going. In many ways, it was fun being with other boys and girls and hanging out in the church and parish events.

One day Dad and I travelled from Brooklyn to the Cathedral of St. John the Divine on Amsterdam Avenue in Manhattan. I was startled at how huge the unfinished cathedral was. It is a tenth of a mile long and 126 feet high. It was dark and gloomy inside the stone walls and pillars. We walked around to the catafalque of a bishop. An effigy of his body lay on top. I was frightened. Death? Was a body really there or in there?

When I was eleven, Dad gathered ten kids into a Confirmation Class. Dixie Haas and Virginia Mazza were in the class. They were pretty girls and I liked being near them.

We had to learn and recite The Lord's Prayer, the Apostles' Creed, and The Ten Commandments. The Bishop came on May 4, 1942. He was tall, handsome, and wore gorgeous vestments. He solemnly said some prayers, laid his hands on our heads, and we were confirmed as full members of the Christian Church, Episcopal branch. I was excited at the event. I received some gifts. That excitement was the only emotional experience. I did not feel any closer to God or Jesus.

Over the next three years we moved a couple of times and attended local churches and went to Sunday School. Dad at that time was not working as a parish priest.

At Holy Trinity Church in the East New York Borough of Brooklyn, I became a member of St. Vincent's Guild for acolytes. We had regular meetings at the church to learn the intricate steps for the more complex liturgies at that church. It was fun. There were nice older boys who conducted the meetings. One was Robert Wellner. He was employed as a machinist working metals. He decided he wanted to be a priest of the Episcopal Church. He went on to

Rutgers University and on to seminary and was ordained. I was impressed with his interest and desire for ordination. I still wanted to join the Army Air Corps.

We went to Manhattan to the Church of St. Mary the Virgin on 46th Street. It was an acolytes' festival and there were boys from all over New York City dressed in their red or black cassocks with white cottas wearing the red-ribboned St. Vincent's Guild silver medal. The procession of all the boys and clergy was grand and lengthy. The church was filled with the smoke from the incense. We all took communion together. The church was huge and impressive. I remember it was thrilling to see so many acolytes and clergy, and so much smoke. I have never forgotten the experience.

One time I was in a class on the Ten Commandments taught by a laywoman from Holy Trinity. We came to the 7th, "Thou shalt not commit adultery." I sort of knew what that meant. She simply said, "Married men or women should not have sex with anyone else but their spouses." Simple and straightforward. Later in life, my disregard for this commandment ruined my first marriage. The only other thing I remember from that class was to learn the colors used for the altar hangings during the church year. Purple for Advent, gold for Christmas, purple for Epiphany, purple for lent, gold for Easter and green for the Pentecost season. I thought all this stuff was kind of interesting.

In 1945, I enrolled in St. Paul's School in Garden City, New York. It was an Episcopal School and we had daily chapel to begin the day. The chapel pews faced each other, choir-style. Up five steps from the floor was a sanctuary with maroon carpeting. A gold cross sat atop a seven-foot wide altar. On the right facing the altar was a small pipe organ with a gentle sound. On the left was a wooden pulpit. There was a brown solid wood chair for the officiant and a prayer desk in front of it. Light filled the room from tall gothic pointed windows.

The daily service was led by a student or a teacher. We sang a hymn; there was a brief reading from the Bible, some prayers, and a final hymn. Sometimes the headmaster or the chaplain gave a short address. I liked the service. As the boys and teachers filed out, the organist played a voluntary of quiet music, subtly interweaving the majestic tones with a line from popular music like *I'm Always Chasing Rainbows* or *Blue Skies Smiling at Me,* I enjoyed this playful interchange between the sacred and the secular. During my senior year, I often led the morning service.

The classes were straightforward: English, Latin, Math, Science, History, and French or Spanish. We had lots of homework and study halls scattered through the day. I played football, basketball, and baseball during the four years I was at the school. I really enjoyed the sports program.

I went to church regularly at the Cathedral of the Incarnation in Garden City or at home in our local St. Thomas Church, Bushwick Avenue, or Holy Trinity, Arlington Avenue, both in Brooklyn. I received communion and attended because that is what we did. There was no pressure from Mother or Dad. I suppose church-going was gently becoming part of who I was, but I did not feel any jolt of religious awareness. I did begin to enjoy the sacred music, cantatas, choruses, and singing the hymns.

During my high school summers, I went to the Episcopal Church Camp DeWolfe, named after our Bishop. It was in Wading River on Long Island. We went to Eucharist every day and had prayers in the evening. There was Bible, and other religious studies that I endured. We had to get through them so we could swim, play baseball, and eat.

We were introduced to *The Practice of Religion.* That book was the basis of learning how to pray, prepare to make a confession of sins, prepare to take communion, and to be more mindful of actually taking the bread and wine as symbols of the body and blood of Jesus. I was really interested in following these steps and practices. It deepened my intellectual understanding of the church services I attended. However, while I thought practices improved my understanding and awareness, I did not feel much emotion about it all.

The most important part of my religious consciousness was meeting the clergy who were our counselors, teachers, and chaplains while we were at camp. The camp director, Fr. John, and his wife Betty were expert dancers. They did the tango with the grace and passion of Latins. They danced a ferocious jitterbug, Fr. John in his clerical collar. Fr. Capon whittled sticks and told interesting stories and introduced me to the writings of H.H. Munro.

Fr. Kupsch was fat and jolly and quite profoundly reverent when saying the mass in the outdoor chapel overlooking Long Island Sound from the top of the bluff on which the camp rested. The green of the trees framed the blue-green waters of the Sound.

When I was a college student I became the waterfront director of the camp. I taught swimming and was the lifeguard when the children went swimming.

By the early 50s the civil rights movement was rising. At Camp, Fr. Fergus Fulford, a very black priest, was at camp for a week or two. He described what it was like for him to be a black in the south, where he grew up. The indignities of his having to make way for white people when walking on the sidewalk. He told of being called "nigger" and "boy" even when he was an adult, a graduate student, and an ordained priest. It was difficult or impossible for him to vote, or to get a hotel room or a seat in a restaurant. He told these stories with a mixture of wit and anger.

I had read about these stories. But here was a human being, a priest, someone I loved and respected, who told us these things happened to him. I felt powerful feelings of outrage and fury. I often think this was my conversion emotional religious experience.

In group discussions at camp we talked about the teachings of Jesus about justice and care for the poor and the sick. I finally got the point that being a Christian, a follower of Jesus, meant that we are to do something about the outrageous way African-Americans are treated in the United states of America and around the world.

One of my best friends at camp was Richard. He was planning to attend seminary, and was very pious, saying prayers and wearing a cross on the outside of his shirt. He and I were in charge of eight youngsters at a meal table. Richard would grab whatever food he wanted and pile it on his plate. Then the rest of us got what was left. I finally confronted him and said, "I thought we Christians were to share what we have. How come you grab the food first?" He heard me. From then on, he passed the food first to the kids and then took his.

Another priest at camp was Fr. Welty. One day we sat in the living room of the main house of the camp. It was a warm afternoon with breezes wafting in from the Sound. He was born and raised in the south. Tall and slender, he spoke with a strong southern accent. He too saw the injustice black Americans faced in our country. He said, "A popular jibe at this time by race haters was, 'Would you want your daughter to marry one?' Many people thought that a white woman marrying a black man horrible." Fr. Welty had a 12-year-old blonde daughter. He said, "If my girl wanted to marry a black man, that would be all right with me. However, I would warn them that they would face a difficult future, but that is all I'd say." Again, I was moved by Fr. Welty's humanity and openness.

During the two summers I was waterfront director of Camp DeWolfe, the clergy and staff read Morning and Evening Prayer from the Book of Common Prayer of the Episcopal Church. We sat on the porch of the main house in reed chairs. We sat in a circle and looked out on the waters, the leaves on the trees, and lawns. We stayed quiet for a while and then we read a Psalm or two, listened to an Old Testament and New Testament reading, and the leader read us the beautiful prayers in that book. I did enjoy the twice-daily practice, but I often found it interruptive of other things I was interested in doing. They were mainly flirting with the girls and reading.

I liked the regularity of those daily "offices" as they were called. I listened to the readings from the Bible and prayers. I grew to love and enjoy the stories of Moses, Abraham, David, and Solomon. The pictures of Jesus and the travels of Paul all were food for our discussions afterward. We did not take the stories literally, we loved them as lore.

In 1948, my grandmother Cromey died. She was buried in a casket in a cemetery in Brooklyn. It was a cold rainy day, the sky gray and then darkening. Driving away under the green trees along the slick pavement, I thought, "How awful to leave Grandma here in the cold ground all alone." We had lived with her and my late Grandpa Cromey since 1945. Her death was not unexpected. I felt really sad about the frightening power of death, its loneliness. Is she in heaven? Is she just dead and that was it? Nothing? As a church-going Episcopalian of seventeen I assumed there was life after death.

Those views and others were challenged at New York University in Greenwich Village in New York City. I studied English and Philosophy, along with French, math, biology, and the usual range of academic courses.

Mr. Edwards, an instructor in Philosophy, took us through the traditional Thomas Aquinas articles of belief in God and then demolished them as illogical. I was fascinated by the arguments and the discussions which followed. He invited the class to his apartment where we argued more, drank wine, and he sold us his extra books. He spoke precisely with a German accent. He was short and thin, humorous, and open to other opinions. I felt challenged but mostly amused at myself because the arguments slid off my thinking. I still went to church.

We had some college chaplains whom I respected. They helped me see that there is a difference between logic and faith. These chaplains' job was not to save our religious beliefs but to make us think about what we truly believed and why.

I took a course in Existentialism with Professor William Barrett, a tall, scholarly, dry, and clever teacher. He took us through the arguments indicating that life had no meaning, it just is. Belief in God and life after death were interesting notions but irrational and unprovable. I loved the courses. I even wrote a paper in Logic and received an A for my efforts. I still went to church on Sundays and sometimes even at times in between.

In grammar school, we had learned about the present and past tense. I had argued that there is no present tense. As soon as you say something in the present tense it is immediately in the past tense. As soon as you say something in the present tense it is immediately past tense. The other kids tried to get me to see there had to be a present tense. Stubborn me, I stuck to the notion that present is immediately the past. Years later I looked back on that discussion to note I had some interest in philosophy.

One day I was an acolyte in a small church in Greenwich Village at an early morning mass. I was staring at the flames of the candlestick on the altar. I noticed the yellow and blues around the wick, I saw the light smoke arise from the flame. My mind went to work and wondered if this was a religious experience or was I just looking and noticing the lighted candle.

I had read about the excitement and emotionalism in fundamentalist churches. Shouting, arm waving, fainting, holy rolling, and snake handlers were expected occurrences. I had heard Episcopalians say they felt the presence of God at the Eucharist, meditation, and prayer. I never had. I thought perhaps I should cook up an ecstatic experience.

Just after my junior year at NYU, Lillian and I married. We began to have regular intercourse. The exquisite pleasure of sex and orgasm hogged my mind. I thought about sex all the time. I began to think of orgasm as an out of body experience. For a moment, the "little death" as the French say, was a spiritual and religious experience. I had experienced the pleasure earlier when I masturbated. But with Lillian the sexual experience was something new and deeper.

I did not think that a personal God was egging me on and entering my life through sex. I did have a sense of profound joy and physical surrender and relief in our sexual contacts. This gave me an inkling of the connection of sex and religious consciousness.

NYU offered intellectual challenges to belief in God as father, all good, all knowing and perfect. That notion of God is inadequate and indefensible. God. God is not a being. God is being itself. God is in and through all of life. He is not a grandfather in the sky checking our sins. God is in everything. Paul Tillich used the expression "God is the ground of being."

In addition, God resides in the inexpressible. Love, wonder, nature, thrill, art, music, sculpture, painting, theater, and dance all produce a sense of things not seen.

Seminary: Fall of 1953

Fifty of us entered our first year at The General Theological Seminary in the Chelsea district of New York City. We began a three-year course of study preparing us for the priesthood in the Episcopal Church. We left the bustle of 9th Avenue and entered the green lawn with its trees and flowers and calm of the seminary close, a word that means campus in our parlance. The brick dormitories, classrooms, Chapel, and dining hall were reminiscent of the Oxford and Cambridge colleges in England. The seminary is a place of prayer, study, and the development of our religious lives.

Lectures in Old and New Testament, Theology, Ethics, Church History, Music, and Pastoral Theology gave us a rich grounding in the history, worship and thinking of the Christian religion. Tutorials with faculty members gave plenty of time to discuss and think through what we believed and thought, and how we behaved. Homework was massive, papers abundant, examinations difficult, and the atmosphere was that of rigorous learning. Beliefs and practices of the church and ethics were extended over discussions at meals and among the students.

The chapel sits in the center of the close. Its tower stands tall over all the buildings of the seminary and those surrounding the square block of the seminary. Bells sound from the tower, summoning us to services in the high-ceilinged interior filled with stained glass windows of biblical stories. The high altar at the far end has a statue of Jesus as the Good Shepherd surrounded by his disciples. Huge carved stalls go a third of the way up the walls with seats for the faculty, students, and guests. The space is dark and conducive to individual and corporate worship.

The student body attended services in the morning and the evening. We were taught to meditate. I failed meditation. I either fell asleep or thought about sex or when would this damned exercise be over? I went through the motions of the services. I said the prayers and listened to the Bible readings. I often was moved by the organ music and the burring sound of 150 men's voices chanting the psalms or singing the hymns.

In 1954 during my second year in Seminary the U.S. Supreme Court, in Brown vs. Ferguson, ended segregation in public schools. Most of the faculty and students and I rejoiced in the decision. However, I was astonished that some of the men condemned it. My judgmental self said, "How could professed Christians not rejoice that black students could get better educations?" I was disheartened by their attitudes.

My religious consciousness developed as I learned so much about religion and its history. I enjoyed the studies, particularly as they related to real life, thinking, and behavior. I enjoyed participating in the liturgy. l looked forward to saying the Eucharist, preaching, baptizing, marrying, and burying the dead. The life of a priest and pastor was a good life that I looked forward to entering. There would be the responsibilities of administration of a church building, a community of people, and teaching the young and old.

The rector or pastor of a church makes his own schedule and is responsible to a monthly meeting of the vestry and must turn up on Sundays and for scheduled events. Clergy have great freedom over their time and what they choose to take on. Very few jobs or professions have that freedom. I took the responsibility seriously. I confess that I did not work very hard. I am an efficient person and well organized so I got a lot done in a short time. I had a lot of free time for family, fun, rest, and reading.

In my first jobs as a priest in New York, I worked a lot with teens and early college students. I played the role of being a regular fellow, laughing, joking, and teasing the kids, yet I wanted them also to see me as a serious Christian. Lillian and I had teens from the parishes as our baby-sitters. The girls particularly would come to the rectory and take our children for a walk or just play with them in the house.

However, I made it clear that I was the priest-celebrant at the services. I always wore my collar. At teen conferences, I would always show up first in the daily morning chapel service to show that I was practicing the prayer life I talked about. I certainly did this to show off my piety. It did not go very deep. However, I did like being a role model. I did want the kids to be comfortable in the church, to love and enjoy the liturgy and to learn about God and Jesus.

In 1962, we moved to San Francisco. I and other clergy were confronted with the civil rights movements for African Americans. These years and events drove home for me the teachings of Jesus that we Christians were to feed the hungry, welcome the stranger, heal the sick, and seek for justice. Black Americans faced massive racial discrimination in restaurants, hotels, travel, and voting and were often in poverty. Martin Luther King, Jr., in his speeches and action made plain the connection between the teachings of Jesus, the Bible, and social action to change injustices to people.

With all this ferment, there was an outbreak of glossolalia, or speaking in tongues, in some Episcopal Churches. A friend and classmate in the seminary was Jerry, who said he felt filled with the Holy Spirit and could speak in tongues. I had heard some people speaking in tongues and it sounded like babble to me. Even Jerry said it sounded like babble but he felt the presence of God when the tongues took over his consciousness. I tried a couple of times to meditate and wished for the power to speak in tongues. It never worked for me. I take the view that if the activity means something to the believer and it is not harmful, then they should pursue it. I lost all interest in the subject. I heard little of glossolalia over the decades that followed. My mind was on other things anyway.

I was inspired to thought and action by James Baldwin's *The Fire Next Time*. Soon Dr. King called on the clergy to descend on Selma, Alabama, to march for freedom for black Americans. Several of us clergy went. I felt this was a holy crusade. I felt God called us to act to help end gross injustice.

As I celebrated the Eucharist and preached sermons, I really felt I was doing what the Bible, Jesus, and the Christian Church were all about. Many people said they were wounded and hurt that their clergy took these strong positions favoring black Americans. I saw that in order to free some Americans, others would be hurt and perhaps leave the church.

The issue of hurt turned to outrage when some other clergy and I began to support rights for Lesbians and Gays. Many church people regarded homosexuality as sinful, bad, and wrong. Some of us getting to know a number of LGBT people as human beings saw that they were just born as people loving people of the same sex. The outrage went further when we advocated that same sex couples should be able to marry in the church. The Bible was quoted erroneously that God hated gays. Lots of Biblical scholars pointed out that certain passages could not be taken as God's law and needed historical context and explanation.

Walking on picket lines and appearing in protest demonstrations were religious, spiritual, or Christian experiences. I was moved by the suffering and pain I saw in African Americans and LGBT human beings. Was this God speaking to me? I don't really know. It could be the devil. I got no financial gain from these works. A certain amount of notoriety came my way. I enjoyed being seen on TV and having my picture and writing appear in newspapers. These were pleasant rewards.

As time went on I was involved in the anti-Vietnam war demonstrations, the women's and anti-war movements. My wife Ann is passionate about nature, the wilderness, birds, and all things outdoors. I notice that my concerns were more directly concerned with people. I have little concern about the great problems of the environment. I cheer those people who do.

Many people say that concerns for the civil and human rights of others and for nature are spiritual issues. I suppose they are. These issues deal with the welfare of people and the planet, which are all gifts to us from God.

I believe that I am a religious person as a gift to me from God. I did not earn or deserve my interest and devotion to religion. It just is. I have increased and developed that religious interest by attending seminary for three years, working for the church, and reading and worshipping.

Here is what I do as a religious person. I attend church every Sunday, missing a few once in a while when on vacation. I prefer worshipping in the context of the Eucharist. I am not fond of readings or prayers as the best way for me to participate in corporate worship. However, I do enjoy a good sermon that is well prepared, and illustrated with good stories that move me emotionally. Most sermons I hear are pretty thin.

I pray on the run, when walking, swimming, on awaking, before sleeping, and whenever I feel like it. My prayers are almost all thanksgivings for my wife, children, family, and life. I pray for the healing of those who are sick, hungry, homeless, in prison, or any other need. I do not expect God to come running to my aid. Remembering others in need reminds me that I may be called on to give direct help, like sending money, cards or visiting the sick.

I even envy those who have a set time and place to read the Bible, say prayers and meditate. I have tried them all and none suit me. So I pray on the run.

I often think that I am not a very deep person. I don't feel very holy or religious. I have never had a powerful specifically religious experience. Actually, I am quite happy with who I am. I just notice there are areas of my life where I am dissatisfied and want to learn more but do not want to work too hard at the learning.

There is a hymn we sing in church. Each verse begins with the words "God is love." Does that mean that love is God? God is love has Biblical roots and is a common expression in preaching, prayer, and discussions of God. Love is probably the basic emotion and concept that undergirds all our human relations. Yet we are part of an unloving world. War, racism, homophobia, and injustice are rampant in a loving world.

Love is a powerful element. A mother's love for her child is full of love but also almost absolute desire to protect the child at any cost. We say love is eternal, yet people divorce. We can grow to hate our sons or daughters if they become cruel and inhuman.

The best we can do really is to be satisfied with intimations of God in the experience of others and in ourselves. "God is love" is really a good intimation. The power and intimacy of love between people, adults, children, and neighbors makes us feel a reaching beyond ourselves. Love is its own power.

Here is where I find God:

1. In worship—Those of us who attend church regularly hear the Bible read and hymns sung whose words are all about God, Jesus, the Holy Spirit, and all the traditional ideas and traditions of religious Christianity down through the ages. That past becomes part of us. I am glad I worship in that long line of Christians to the time of Jesus and back beyond that in the traditions and faith of Judaism. When I receive the blessed bread and wine, I often feel a connection not only to Jesus at the last supper, but to everyone else at the church that day and my family and friends.

2. In Social Justice—In the fight for freedom for all people, especially African-Americans, homosexuals, women, all people of color, and all those enslaved, comes a profound sense of righteousness. Freedom is the way things ought to be. There is a rightness about the quest for freedom for all. There is a powerful religious and emotional dimension in helping others to become free.

3. In art—When I first saw Michelangelo's statue of David in Florence, I was shocked at how moved I was. That gorgeous statue was created out of a slab of marble. I felt astonishment at the beauty of that sculpture I am happy to call an intimation of God.

4. In community—I love to go to church and be part of a wonderful mix of human beings. The rich and well-dressed next to the transsexual in a red miniskirt, the lady with the hat next to the woman too heavy to get out of her wheelchair, the man in dreadlocks next to the crewcut man in tight jeans, the woman in denim jeans reading a scripture lesson. In the

80s and 90s we worshipped with men who had HIV disease, skinny bodies, Kaposi's Sarcoma scabs, young men on canes, and so many caring for them. We all took the sacrament of Holy Communion together, had coffee together. Then we visited many in the hospital and we buried them when they died. In this joyous and terror-filled and loving and forgiving community, I get a sense of God.

5. Awe—When I was a therapist and counselor, many times I helped a client see something, get the meaning of something, an awareness or an insight. It may have come from thinking together, but suddenly there was a jump into some clarity. It was "awesome" to use the popular slang. It was inspiring. It seemed to come from nowhere.

6. In music—the first time I heard Berlioz' *Symphony Fantastique*, the horns were placed behind us in the symphony hall. At the tuba mirum, the horns blared gorgeously behind us, catching us by surprise. I was in awe. It created powerful sudden emotions in me. I shuddered. Another time as I was listening to Tchaikovsky's *1812 Overture* I began to weep as the music crashed and then sounded sweetly.

7. Emotions—The wide variety of human emotions catch us by surprise. Raging anger, sweet happiness, groping sadness, fearsome sexuality, and jolting fear enter our consciousness uninvited. They appear out of nowhere, are hard to control and need nurturing.

8. Sex—Sexual intercourse is at the same moment the most giving and receiving expression of love and pleasure. The moment of orgasm is a living and a dying. The intimacy of talk, humor, and honesty after sex may be the most intimate moments in all of life.

9. In nature—The beauty of nature, mountains, trees, forests, deserts, and the sky give some people a sense of the divine. The complexity, habits and colorful beauty of animals, birds, mammals, and fish bring a sense of awe and wonder to many.

10. In the power of the mind—The human capacity to think, evaluate, calculate, analyze, memorize, and meditate is so complex and surprising that it reflects the magnitude of the universe.

11. In the Joke—The trick of getting a joke seems miraculous. Some people have it, some are slow, and some never get it.

12. The power of people's faith—Many people have faith in God, Jesus, and Allah. Millions upon millions of people have faith in the divine. Most never question the existence of God or worry about evidence, arguments, and those who don't believe. They just believe. When the planes plowed into New York buildings, people were so shocked they poured into churches, many to pray. In times of turmoil, pain and destruction, people pray.

13. Thanksgiving—A trait that most people have is to be thankful. Some are thankful to God or to the universe. Others are thankful for the economy, the country, and their families. The desire to give thanks is an intimation of the divine.

14. Grace—Many of us are thankful for unearned gifts. The powerful love that one person can have for another is a gift. No one earns his or her partner. He or she is a gift. Many people ascribe their wealth and status as the result of hard work and…luck. Thomas Edison worked for hours to perfect the light bulb. Then one day by luck he found the right element for the filament and his invention was complete.

The aha moment that comes to actors, authors, inventers, and business people are intimations of God.

I end this section with some of the words of one of my favorite hymns

Immortal, Invisible, God only wise,
in light inaccessible hid from our eyes,
most blessed most glorious, the Ancient of days, almighty,
victorious, thy great Name we praise.

Thy justice like mountains high soaring above,
Thy clouds, which are fountains of goodness and love.

All laud we would render, O help us to see
'tis only the splendor of light hideth thee.

Hymn 423 in the 1982 Episcopal Hymnal, Words by Walter Chalmers Smith (1824-1906) Hymn tune St. Deniol.

God as a hint in all these areas

God as a hint in all these areas is a God I can focus on, worship and reflect upon.

After years of mulling over these ideas, I can write now what Joseph Campbell once said. Asked whether he believed in God, Campbell replied, "I know a good myth when I see one." I take that to mean that using the word God reflects a mythology of God as creator, sustainer, and redeemer, and ever-present.

When I say I believe in God, that is a personal and pastoral way of referring to the ground of all being, that God is being itself. It is hard to relate to the ground of all being or being itself. The word God reflects the great Jewish idea of the creator God who enters human history in actions like the parting of the Red Sea, and for Christians in the man Jesus.

I need to relate to God on a personal and prayerful level. I give thanks to God for all the blessings of my life, wife, children, grandchildren, friends, and family. I am thankful for food, a home, and a safe country. I may ask God to grant me a safe flight. I do not expect God to intervene and hold the plane up if it gets mechanical problems. The prayer works on me, it gives me a sense of safety. But my prayer does not work on God.

I do not call myself a Christian much anymore. A follower of Jesus is what I prefer. Too many Christians are hateful, narrow, prejudiced, cruel, and exclusionary. My leader and inspiration is Jesus. He called on his followers to feed the hungry, heal the sick, and visit those in prison. He calls us to love and forgive our neighbors, ourselves, and our enemies. He spoke against injustice. I do my best to follow Jesus' teachings. My life works best that way. Pope Francis said recently that churches the do not feed the poor should be taxed. I agree with that.

Many Christian friends belong to and support their churches and denominations which discriminate against homosexuals, women, and same-sex marriages.

Many of my Christian friends mock, degrade, scorn, and deride Donald Trump. Yes, Jesus got angry and did some name-calling. He did not have a perfect moral life. He also did not participate in elections.

I don't think mocking and degrading help win elections. Campaign managers think some negative ads do help candidates.

I choose to support, encourage, seek the truth, and contribute to Hilary Rodham Clinton.

I think her experience in government, as Senator and Secretary of State and her common sense would have made her a good President. She was also the wife of the President for eight years.

The government can only accomplish help for the poor, adequate health care, control of blatant and cruel capitalism. I will support policies that work toward those ends. I think the Democratic Party, with all its flaws, can best accomplish those ends.

Metaphysical Illumination

Our friends who are scientific, atheists, or have no interest in religion make me think about what I believe about God and religion.

I am happy to call myself religious of the Christian Episcopalian persuasion. I have doubts and am open to discussion and examination of my faith, thinking and beliefs.

I call myself religious because I sense that there is so much in the people, the world, and the universe that give me awe and wonder. I am breathless at the "vast expanse of interstellar space, galaxies, suns, the planets in their courses and this fragile earth, our island home" as our Book of Common Prayer reads.

All this stands before me and moves me. To repeat, I stand in "awe and wonder." Men and women of science explore all aspects of this universe, the world, and the people in it. Medicine and psychiatry delve into the intricacies of our bodies and minds. Physics, mathematics, and computers help us understand the working of the world better. Astronomers lead us in exploring interstellar space. Governments and political science attempt to organize our political lives.

Religious people explore the holy, sacred, or divine dimensions of life. They don't get explored easily. Logic and reason can help. Religious perceptions are deeply personal.

Many religious people testify that they have had a personal encounter with God, Jesus, the Holy Spirit, or some force beyond themselves. Southern Baptists believe that this spiritual experience is necessary for salvation.

The Old and New Testaments of The Bible hold many stories of religious experience. Sometimes it happens in dreams or walking along a road or in the face of injustice. "The Idea of the Holy" by Rudolf Otto describes many reports of a Mysterium Tremens, a mystical experience described as holy, somehow connected to God or a divine source. I suggest that the proliferation of religion throughout the world is rooted in some kind of mystical experience.

True confession time. I am religious but have not ever had a

Mysterium Tremens or mystical experience. I am religious because I always have been, I like going to church and am comforted by the Eucharist, the prayers of thanksgiving, the singing and community. I was brought up in a family that went to church on Sundays and said a prayer at dinner. My father was a priest. My parents read Bible stories to my brother and me. Going to church on Sundays was as natural and normal as eating breakfast. I am a follower of Jesus. I follow his call to care for the poor, the sick, and those seeking justice.

People can be religious without a special mystical event or metaphysical illumination.

Here are several patterns:

- You went to church as a child, gave it up in college, married and had a child and went back to church as the child grew.

- You left the church of your childhood, then married a religious person and went to church with him or her.

- You faced the death of a parent, spouse, or child and found comfort again in religion.

- You came back to church when diagnosed with HIV disease.

- You, like me, always went to church.

- You felt close to God or had a near mystical experience when you were out in nature, hearing great music, viewing great paintings or sculpture. I certainly felt powerfully moved when I first saw Michelangelo's David in Florence, Italy.

- You were moved by visiting sacred spaces: St. Paul's Cathedral in London, St. Peter's in the Vatican, Notre Dame in Paris, the Cologne Cathedral in Germany.

- You proudly proclaim you are spiritual but not religious (SBNR). I suspect spiritual is the word you use to separate from a religious path you now reject.

- You regard sexual intercourse and sexual intimacy resulting in orgasm as mystical. There is a sense of complete oneness with the other partner that is mysterious and touches the divine. In the sex act one is completely selfish and self-giving at the same moment. There is mutual joy.

- You have used certain drugs that produce what are called mystical experiences. LSD for some produces profound mental, physical, and emotional experiences which the taker may describe as seeing God or having a sense of the divine.

- You participate in certain types of dancing like whirling and leaping that can produce mystical states.

Summing up

I just can't pray to the "ground of all being" and "God as being itself." The philosophy and theology are fine. But how to pray? I now pray to God, the father. I wish I could say God the mother. That does not work for me. I wish it did. It will work for many other men and women.

God the father is personal, intimate, a being to whom I can pray. Father means creator, symbol of love and forgiveness. When I pray now to my God, I know God means so much more than a divine parent. But now I can pray to and worship a personal God, a metaphor for the "ground of all being." I also am thankful that God has given me this gift of knowing God.

In liberal and scientific circles being religious is not popular and even frowned upon.

However, religion is alive and healthy and will always be with us and with our spirits.

CHAPTER 14

MY PART IN THE LGBT RIGHTS MOVEMENT

Over the years I have told about my participation in the LGBT rights movement in interviews with scholars, journalists, radio and TV commentators. In this memoir, I plan to write a more complete chronology and report of my activities and those of others I knew in the movement. Along the way I will reflect and comment on the rights movement, the church's reaction, and my personal satisfaction with this important activity. The unique part of this effort is that I am a straight person, not gay, and a priest of the Episcopal Church. The usual questions asked me were: Why did you get involved in gay rights though you are straight? What does you church think of your involvement with gay people? Isn't the Bible against homosexual activity?

I will answer the usual questions right off and get them behind me. I am a straight man and felt the LGBT rights movement was a justice issue not a sexual one. I was active in the civil rights activities for African Americans. The gay rights movement also was a justice issue for a persecuted minority.

What did the church think about my involvement? Some people thought it was fine, others thought I was crazy, gay, or deluded. Officials in the church never did anything official against me.

The Bible appears to say some negative things about homosexual activity. I am not a Biblical literalist. Those passages must be looked at in light of the date, the context in which they were uttered, and the prejudices of people at the time they were written. None of them are the inspired word of God. Nothing in the Bible is God almighty talking to us directly. Obviously fundamentalist, literalist, and very conservative readers of the Bible would disagree. But "frankly Scarlet, I don't give a damn."

I have kept a scrapbook of clippings from newspapers and magazines, which mention my name in connection with gay rights. I use that as a source of the chronology. However, I have memories from teen, college, seminary years, and from my first jobs before I began to speak publicly about homosexual issues. I will depend on my memories for a large part of what I write.

In August of 1963, I preached a sermon in Grace Cathedral, San Francisco. At that time, I held the exalted title of "executive assistant" to the Episcopal Bishop of California, James Albert Pike. At 31 years old, I had the privilege of being associated with one of my heroes. Bishop Pike was an outstanding liberal who drew direct connections between the gospel of Jesus and daily life. He spoke out on issues of the time, supporting birth control, and opposing communist witch-hunts and attempts to limit free speech. As his assistant, I was a Canon of Grace Cathedral in San Francisco. A canon is a priest on the staff of the diocese and cathedral.

It was the first time and only time the Dean of the Cathedral ever invited me to preach at Grace.

In the sermon, I said we must treat homosexuals as human beings, learn the complexities of homosexual behavior, be open and loving, become friends with gay people. Do not treat them as a class but as individuals.

The Gospel for the day spoke of the Christian concern for the outcasts. It occurred to me that homosexuals were not only outcasts but also invisible. I pointed out that they were a silent minority in the church, ignored except as financial donors. If the sexual orientation of a gay priest became public, it was thought necessary to have him removed from his position. That sermon of mine was also patronizing: I naively suggested that homosexuals needed psychological help, but I did call for love, compassion, and forgiveness.

I don't remember any negative feedback from members of the church that Sunday. As a result of the sermon I was invited to appear on a couple of radio stations for interviews. One was with Owen Span with KGO radio. He broadcast from a bar and restaurant in the financial district. I was nervous and don't remember one thing I said that time.

I received one letter from a gay man who wrote. "Sometimes I go into a church when it is deserted and fall on my knees and weep, not so much for my sins but because I am overcome with despair. This lack of hope is what keeps me from church, I suppose, although sometimes I get an overwhelming desire to worship God, even though I often feel I must be already damned by Him."

Not long after that I met Joe Allison of the *S.F. News Call Bulletin*. We were in the men's room at Westlake Joe's restaurant. He asked me who I was and we began to chat. Later, he interviewed me for his column, "The Last Angry Man." His article appeared on September 13, 1963. In it I was quoted as saying, "Our attitude generally is that people with this psychic and emotional condition are some kind of animal despised of man and God and not worthy of human concern.... They seem to be too much of a threat to our own sexuality—so we despise or even worse ignore the community."

In addition to my interest in gay rights, I was deeply engaged in the civil rights movement. In the spring of 1964, major civil rights groups called for picketing protesting the hiring policies of the automobile show rooms along Van Ness Avenue, or Auto Row.

One Saturday afternoon, I took my oldest daughter Leigh to walk with me. A lovely picture of her holding my hand, walking on the picket line appeared in the San Francisco Chronicle.

Later several of us clergy sat-in on April 11. We were among 250 people arrested that day. Movie actor Sterling Hayden was among the group. There was enormous media attention paid to us. The clergy got out of jail the same afternoon. We were convicted and fined for trespassing. The students at The Church Divinity School of the Pacific paid our fines.

In 1965, answering the call to clergy from Martin Luther King, Jr., several of us clergy from the Bay Area went to Selma, Alabama. After the first march had been brutally dispersed by police, arousing national indignation, he asked us to join him in the next march from Selma to Montgomery.

Gay Rights

One day in 1964 while I was working with Bishop Pike in his office, he handed me a letter addressed to him and he said, "Please answer this and say decline. But maybe you'd be interested in attending and representing me."

I was and I did. It was a weekend conference for clergy and homosexuals to be held at the Ralston-White Retreat Center in Mill Valley just over the Golden Gate Bridge in Mill Valley. It was a dialogue set up to discover our mutual humanity. Gay and lesbian leaders felt the clergy could be valuable allies in the gay rights movement if we got to know each other. We listened to each other's stories, our lives, goals, and ambitions.

As I heard of the pain and oppression, as well as the joys and gaiety of homosexuals, I realized here was another oppressed minority, another group of people deprived of their full humanity "in the land of the free and the home of the brave." I realized that gay rights were a civil rights issue also. I remember taking a walk in the woods with Phyllis Lyon and Del Martin. Del said she had thought she would be butch like a man and Phyllis the fem, more like a woman. Then they laughed and said they no longer lived by this stupid stereotype. They were just two women who loved each other and chose to live together.

Out of this group of clergy and gays was founded the Council on Religion and the Homosexual (CRH). Our purpose was to develop dialogue between straights and gays in local churches. We felt that if church people could meet openly gay men and women and speak with them, discover their humanity, then reconciliation and communication would result.

In 1965, several gay groups sponsored a New Year's costume ball with proceeds to go to the council. The police were outraged. The vice squad advised us that we clergy were being used by the gay community. One asked, "Aren't your wives going to be upset by your hanging around with homosexuals?" They even asked us about our theology. They assured us they would make sure that the laws about dinking and unlawful sexual conduct were obeyed.

When we arrived at the event, police photographers took pictures of the 500 people who attended as they were going into the party. The police entered the party looking for lawbreakers. Our lawyers tried to block their entrance, saying it was a private party. Two lawyers were arrested for obstructing justice. When we clergy tried to block the police entrance we were brushed aside and they would not arrest us. Once inside, the police arrested two partygoers for disorderly conduct.

Now we clergy were outraged. Seven of us called a press conference denouncing the police and their discrimination against gays. They would never invade a debutante's ball or Elks Club costume party. We witnessed clear anti-gay discrimination and we decried what we had seen. Later a judge admonished the police for their action, and all charges were dropped against partygoers and lawyers.

The picture of us clergy at a press conference protesting the police behavior has been widely used in LGBT rights displays, publicity and historical exhibitions ever since.

Media attention abounded. Articles by Gerald Adams, Richard Hallgren, Donovan Bess, and Maitland Zane appeared in the San Francisco newspapers. I had a radio program on KGO called "Churchmen Face the Issues" in which I interviewed politicians, clergy, civil rights leaders, and many others. Radio and TV appearances with Jim Dunbar at KGO and other happened regularly for a couple of years.

But things caught up with me. I was part time Director of Urban Work for the Diocese. I was also part time vicar of St. Aidan's Church in San Francisco. Bishop Pike had encouraged other clergy and me to speak out on social, political, and religious issues. He had been doing it for many years and did not want to be the only person doing so. I had spoken out in favor of the farm workers and Cesar Chavez. This offended rich Episcopalians who owned farms. I defended nudity in North Beach bars, saying there are worse sins than toplessness, offending prudish church people. I wrote an article noting discrimination against blacks in private clubs and clergy spending church money to belong to such groups, thus offending Episcopalians who were club members as well as trustees of the Cathedral and the Diocese. All of this was on top of marching in Selma and hobnobbing with homosexuals.

Bishop Pike went on sabbatical leave to Cambridge in England. The Suffragan Bishop Richard Millard was left in charge. He and the council of the diocese decided to end my job as director of Urban Work and hire a stewardship officer. I had a wife and three children now left with a part time salary. Bishop Pike, calling from England, arranged to pay the missing half of my salary from special funds until I could get St. Aidan's to pay me a full salary.

On Sunday, September 26, 1965, a score or so pickets appeared before the morning service at Grace Cathedral. They were mostly members of the movement to win just treatment for homosexual. I and other clergy worked for fairer of gays and Lesbians. We were widely criticized by church leaders for going against the common attitudes about homosexuals held in church and society.

The Living Church, an Episcopal magazine, carried the story to a nationwide audience. The magazine had published an article by me entitled "The Church and the Homosexual" in the mid-sixties.

I quickly turned to my job as vicar of St. Aidan's in the new Diamond Heights neighborhood of San Francisco. I could spend more time there as a parish priest. I continued getting people to be sensitive to the issues and concerns of gay people. We had dinner party outings with members of the church going to gay restaurants which were run by gay people and very welcoming to straight people. We had study groups and speakers on gay rights issues.

I continued to be involved in other public issues. I wrote an article about segregation in much-publicized debutante balls, jazz in church services, and segregation in the San Francisco public schools. I also testified in a trial where I thought the use of marijuana was justified in religious practices just as alcohol is used in the church's sacrament. The defendant lost.

I joined other clergy in supporting gays who were discriminated against in the military who discharged soldiers and sailors just because they were gay.

In 1967, I spent six weeks as a Fellow of the College of Preachers in Washington, D.C., which helped clergy fashion and improve their preaching. While at the college I was interviewed by a journalist from Newsweek. We met in the fine library of the college, a photographer took pictures and we talked for an hour.

Newsweek Magazine of February 13, 1967 devoted a long article on God and the Homosexual. It described the development of our Council on Religion and the Homosexual (CRH). The article mentioned that I had been "severely criticized by members of the Diocesan Council of California over identifying with the homosexuals' problems."

It is true that I wanted the church to go beyond conventional moral judgments. I believe that the sex act is morally neutral. I also believe that two people of the same sex can express love and deepen that love by sexual intercourse. If two people of the same sex have a loving responsible relationship with each other, they have an obligation to express that love in whatever way they deem appropriate.

It was gratifying to see more and more articles about homosexuality in major newspapers during the late 60s. Not only the San Francisco

Chronicle and Examiner but also the N.Y. Times, Wall Street Journal, and Chicago Daily News.

In 1970, I resigned as Vicar of St. Aidan's Church, San Francisco. I set up a private practice as a California licensed Marriage and Family Therapist. Though no longer having a bully pulpit, I kept up my interest and involvement in LGBT right and civil rights for all minorities.

In the early 1970s I lead a series of Encounter Groups for gay men in the offices of SIR, the Society for Individual Rights on Mission Street. The groups urged men to tell their stories, fear, anxieties, and dreams. I asked them to role-play telling their parents that they were gay. They men told of their fears of losing their jobs, apartments, family, and friends if they found out they were gay. There were not many places in those days where men could tell their stories.

Del Martin and Phyllis Lyon invited me to attend a meeting of the Daughters of Bilitis held at their home. I was plenty nervous. Fifteen attractive women were there. They had never met a male cleric who was interested in lesbian rights. One woman called herself a lipstick lesbian as she wore conventional women's dresses jewelry, shoes, and hairstyles because she really liked being a woman. She said she was laughed at by some of her sister lesbians because she was not butch. All the women had nothing to say that was good about their experience in the churches they had grown up in. I sure learned a lot from that evening and was honored to be there.

During the 1970s I led many groups on a variety of topics, meeting new friends, dealing with anger and communication skills.

I led a number of workshops on human sexuality using sexually explicit films. I insisted the groups watch film with sex between same gender partners. The straight viewers were often very uncomfortable. The discussions that followed made many of the straight viewers see the rightness of those relationships and the injustice against lesbians and gays.

I spent 1977-78 in Germany working with drug addicts. When I returned I began seeking a job as rector of an Episcopal church. I resumed my private practice.

I approached Jewish Community Center when it advertised for a part time job developing groups for single people. I had done that for Esalen Institute and on my own. In the interview, I was told I would not get the job, as I was not Jewish. I charged that the center had a religious bias. I must say it was rather fun poking fun at my Jewish friends and neighbors. There were a couple of newspaper articles.

In October of 1981 I was elected rector of Trinity Episcopal Church at Bush and Gough Streets in San Francisco. I was elected to bring in more people, money, and programs. My marketing plan was to reach out to the LGBT community and single and divorced straight people. Few churches had that agenda in 1981. I spoke a couple of time to the then G-40 group, PFLAG and I was known from my activism in the 60s.

I had a lot of friends in the church who were delighted I was to a rector again. Many people from my private practice were happy for me. My many gay and lesbian friends were also supportive. In December of 1981, some 500 people showed up at Trinity for my installation as rector.

In my sermon when I was installed as rector, I announced that Trinity was going to be a welcoming church to the LGBT community. There was some criticism and much support for my views.

With a mighty pulpit, and ready hand at writing letters to the editor and articles for newspapers and magazines, I continued my support for LGBT rights in church, society, and civil law.

I supported Peter Tachel's efforts outing Church of England Bishops and priests in 1994. I had regularly urged gays and lesbians to out themselves as a way of freeing themselves and move through the self-hatred that afflicted many homosexuals. One lesbian said it was harder to tell her mother that she was a churchgoing Episcopalian than to tell her she was a lesbian.

NOTES

From a friend who read just a section of this:

Utterly fascinating, Robert. Thank you for sending these paragraphs as well as, of course, your being "there" when doing so was not as easy as it is now.

It is so sad, as well as reflective of the institutional Puny Mind, to be reminded of the self-hate that so many gay and transgendered men and women have. Yearning to be affirmed by ourselves and by the greater society, so many are afraid to take the incremental steps toward standing proudly as worthy members of the Body. What particularly saddened me about K. was that his overwhelming faith in affirmation of Christianity was not strong enough to overcome his fear of affirming himself.

As you know, he held a number of views that, especially with the benefit of hindsight, did not stand the test of time. The fact that he was filled with contradictions, in some ways, made me all the more intrigued by him. His journey was long and his pace was slow, yet he never stopped moving forward at his own pace.

Given his fear of acknowledging his homosexuality to himself and to most others, I still wonder what led him to trust me and to invite me into some of the non-public parts of his life. What I remember most of our times together .... during months of recovery following my 1976 back surgery and heart attack was our conversing about things that matter. Never was there any chatting about the insignificant, and never was the dialogue compromised by any assumptions grounded in his position in life or by my youth.

CPSIA information can be obtained
at www.ICGtesting.com
Printed in the USA
BVHW030737040921
616074BV00005B/93

9 781532 034879